VENTURING·BSA

VENTURER HANDBOOK

BOY SCOUTS OF AMERICA

Table of Contents

Introduction

Welcome to Venturing

Welcome to the most exciting youth-planned, youth-run program around! You will develop new interests, learn new skills, go to interesting new places, conquer many challenges, make new friends, learn and practice leadership, and most of all, have *fun*.

The success of your Venturing crew depends on you. You are an important person. It's sort of like the privilege to vote. If you don't exercise your right to plan, participate in, or lead your crew's programs, you might not have any programs. You could have adults plan and run everything for you, but that wouldn't be any fun, and it certainly wouldn't be your program.

So, get involved. Be active. The more you put into Venturing, the more you will get out of it. One way to develop those new interests, learn new skills, go to interesting places, conquer challenges, and have fun is to earn the Venturing Bronze, Gold, Silver, Ranger, and/or Quartermaster awards.

This guidebook outlines the Venturing advancement process. This book details the requirements for the Bronze, Gold, and Silver awards. For details about the Ranger Award, see the *Ranger Guidebook*, No. 3128. For information on the Quartermaster Award, consult the *Sea Scout Manual*, No. 33239B.

What Is Venturing?

Venturing is the young adult program of the Boy Scouts of America for men and women 14 (who have completed the eighth grade) through 20 years of age. Local community organizations such as professional organizations, churches, and civic groups initiate specific Venturing crews. They do this by matching the interests of young adults with the people and program resources within their own organizations.

For example, a local scuba diving shop could start a Venturing crew and invite young adults interested in high-adventure activities to join. A church might have adults that could provide leadership and program support to a Venturing crew that does service-oriented projects like building Habitat for Humanity houses or working at day-care centers and retirement homes. A Boy Scout troop could organize its own crew for young men and women to enjoy high-adventure activities and to train younger Cub Scouts and Boy Scouts.

The program of the Boy Scouts of America is to provide young adults, through these community organizations, an effective Venturing program designed to build character, promote citizenship, and develop personal and mental fitness. Each crew has the responsibility of achieving this purpose by designing its own program.

That's the factual, *outside* definition of Venturing. Let's look for a moment at Venturing from the inside—at the spirit of Venturing.

1

The Spirit of Venturing

Venturing is a catalyst. It brings together adults and young people, and incredible things have happened and can happen in this coming together. The experiences that can emerge from this group of people is up to the people themselves. The more the individuals in the group ask of themselves and of one another, the more possibilities they have for experiences that they'll carry with them the rest of their lives. For example, a crew in Minnesota organized an activity to go sailing off the coast of Africa. A crew in Houston sent along experiments on a recent space-shuttle mission. A crew in California spent nearly 10,000 hours making the nature trails of Angeles National Forest more accessible to the visually impaired by installing trail posts in Braille to identify the forest's flora and fauna.

When ideas and imagination and dreams combine, there is a reaction. That energy is part of the Venturing spirit.

Venturing is guided discovery. With discovery, you step into the unknown, into new areas. You grow. In Venturing, this discovering is guided. Too often, wonderful energy is simply wasted; it stays on the drawing board. In Venturing, that energy is focused. Ideas do not stay on the drawing board; they happen. You learn how to go from a dream to a reality, to something you actually do.

Venturing is an empowering experience. Most of us have some sense of our abilities and strengths. Maybe we haven't had the opportunity, however, to bring those abilities into the open. Venturing is empowering because people discover things about themselves they never realized before. You might be surprised to learn that you are a good negotiator, creative when it comes to program suggestions, quick to react to a change in circumstances, insightful when it comes to reflecting about an experience—these are the same kinds of abilities necessary in any pursuit.

Perhaps you joined a crew because of a specific interest. You'll have the opportunity to pursue that interest, but you will discover, in the process, much more. It's this "much more" that probably best describes Venturing.

How a Crew Gets Started

It is important to know how your crew got started. Below are the steps that your chartered organization took. By the way, the chartered organization is the organization that actually owns your crew. It could be a religious institution, a club, a business, or another organization.

1. Your chartered organization made a commitment with the Boy Scouts of America to charter a Venturing crew.

2. An organizing committee recruited the Advisors and committee for the crew.

3. The new crew committee went through a new-crew orientation and training.

4. A program capability inventory (PCI), discussed later, was completed with adults from the chartered organization and other interested adults to find out what they could contribute to the crew's program. An example would be that the PCI indicated that one of the adults in the chartered organization was an experienced private pilot and owned his own plane. The committee might ask him if he could provide orientation flights for the new Venturers for their third meeting. The results of the PCI became the basis for planning the first few months of the crew's program (until Venturers could plan their own program).

5. An invitation was sent to young people to attend an open house (the first crew meeting, where potential new Venturers are invited to join the crew; discussed later).

6. Your chartered organization was presented a charter for your Venturing crew by the Boy Scouts of America.

7. Crew officers were elected and trained. Then they began planning and presenting your crew's program.

These steps were designed to give your crew a solid foundation, both from an organizational standpoint and from a view to establishing a Venturing spirit.

RESOURCES

New Crew Fast Start (video)
AV-03V013

The Specific Goals of Venturing

There are four goals for the participant in Venturing:

◆ To gain practical experience

◆ To engage in a program with a variety of activities to encourage the development of the whole person

◆ To experience positive leadership from adult and youth leaders and be given opportunities to take on leadership roles

◆ To have a chance to learn and grow in a supportive, caring, and fun environment

The first goal of a Venturing program is to give you an opportunity to pursue your interest in a way that might not be available in a traditional educational setting. We're talking about firsthand, hands-on experiences with people who work in a particular field or have knowledge of it. Venturing recognizes the difference between *reading* about sailing and *going*

sailing, between *talking* about photography and taking pictures, between *discussing* archaeology and going on an archaeological dig.

The second goal is to lead a life in Venturing that fosters personal, social, and community health. That's why a Venturing crew organizes a program around a variety of personal growth activities. This kind of program helps us to experience more balance in our lives; to take responsibility for others and our community; and to be mentally, emotionally, and physically fit.

The third goal is to learn about leadership from adults who set the example. You will learn about leadership by experiencing outstanding adult leadership and by practicing leadership yourself. With other Venturers, you will run your own crew and exercise your own understanding of leadership.

The fourth goal is to create an environment that encourages growth in yourself, in other Venturers, and in Advisors. This is achieved in a place that is safe, fun, and challenging. Venturing provides opportunities for new experiences and new ideas.

RESOURCES

Venturing
Leader Manual
No. 34655B

Goals

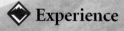 **Experience**

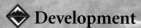 **Development**

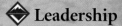 **Leadership**

 Growth

Venturing Insignia Guide

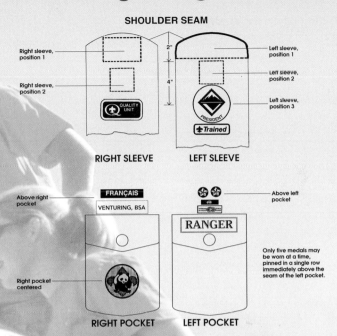

SHOULDER SEAM

Right sleeve, position 1

Right sleeve, position 2

QUALITY UNIT

RIGHT SLEEVE

Left sleeve, position 1

Left sleeve, position 2

Left sleeve, position 3

PRESIDENT

Trained

LEFT SLEEVE

Above right pocket

FRANÇAIS

VENTURING, BSA

Right pocket centered

RIGHT POCKET

Above left pocket

RANGER

Only five medals may be worn at a time, pinned in a single row immediately above the seam of the left pocket.

LEFT POCKET

Venturing Program Identification

VENTURING·BSA

U.S. flag emblem, cloth, red, white, and blue, No. 00103, Venturer and Venturing adult, right sleeve. New uniforms have this emblem already sewn in the correct position.

Shoulder loops, green ribbon, No. 00678, Venturer and Venturing adult, on shoulder epaulets.

Venturing emblem, cloth, No. 04038, Venturer and Venturing adult, right sleeve, position 2 of official uniform shirt.

Council shoulder emblem, cloth, No. 16____ (last three digits indicate the council number), Venturer and Venturing adult, left sleeve, position 1, just below shoulder seam.

Unit number, cloth, white on red, Nos. 10400 through 10408 (last digit indicates the unit number for 0 through 8); for unit number 9, order No. 10406. Venturer or Venturing adult wearing traditional uniform, left sleeve, position 2, touching council shoulder patch. Multiple-digit numerals may be special-ordered—2-digit, No. 10409; 3-digit, No. 10410; 4-digit, No. 10411.

The Venturing Uniform

The recommended uniform is the spruce green Venturing shirt with green epaulette tabs and gray backpacking-style shorts or gray casual pants. However, the uniform, if any, is the choice of the crew. Sea Scouts may wear the Sea Scout uniform. For those crews that choose to have the Venturing uniform, it is recommended to wear it when traveling, at crew meetings, at other Scout meetings, when serving the public, and at other appropriate times. When doing field activities such as sports, water activities, mountaineering, etc., your crew might want to wear something more appropriate to the activity such as the Venturing activity shirt or Venturing T-shirt, both available through the BSA Supply Division.

On dress-up occasions such as a parents' night, open house, or awards ceremony, it is appropriate to wear awards such as the Eagle Scout, Bronze, Gold, Silver, Ranger, and Quartermaster awards.

The green Venturing shirt and tabs and gray shorts are available through the BSA Supply Division.

RESOURCES

Insignia Guide
No. 33066B

Venturing Hand Salute

If a Venturer finds himself or herself in uniform at an occasion where a hand salute is required, Venturers should use the full-hand salute.

Venturing Sign

The Venturing sign is made with a raised right hand with the palm open. The right thumb is slightly open, creating a "V." The elbow is bent at a 90-degree angle.

Activity T-shirt

Activity shirt

BSA High-Adventure Bases

Introduction

The Boy Scouts of America owns and operates three world-class high-adventure bases. They are Philmont in New Mexico, the Northern Tier National High Adventure Programs in Minnesota and Canada, and the Sea Base in the Florida Keys. Each year thousands upon thousands of Scouts, Venturers, and volunteers enjoy the diverse programs offered at these bases.

One of the many programs offered might be a good choice for a new crew's first superactivity since programs offered by high-adventure bases are self-contained. All you have to do is get your crew there and then back home. It doesn't take a lot of expertise to take advantage of one of the national high-adventure programs.

High-adventure base programs are also excellent for experienced crews. You are assured of a safe, quality program, and a program in which there are no surprises. All three bases offer a variety of program selections to match your crew's preferences, ability, and history.

How to Get Information

Brochures and videotapes that describe each high-adventure opportunity are available. Write or call for more information:

Florida National High Adventure Sea Base, P.O. Box 1906, Islamorada, FL 33036, 305-664-4173.

Northern Tier National High Adventure Programs, P.O. Box 509, Ely, MN 55731, 218-365-4811.

Philmont Scout Ranch, Route 1, Four Miles South, Cimarron, NM 87714, 505-376-2281.

Programs Available

Florida National High Adventure Sea Base

A variety of water-related adventures for Scout troops, Venturing crews, and individuals who cannot attend with their crew. There is an additional charge for individuals since the base will provide leadership. Adventures presently include such programs as scuba certification, scuba adventure, a deserted island living experience, a Bahamas adventure, and several sailing experiences (cruises). All programs are exciting and educational. Rates vary and change from time to time. The base offers programs year-round and has a weekend program available October through March. Check the base brochures (produced yearly) for specific details, schedules, and rates. (Scholarships available; employment opportunities available.)

Northern Tier National High Adventure Programs

Wilderness canoeing at its finest can be found at bases located in Ely, Minnesota, and Bissett and Atikokan, Canada. The Northern Tier administrative headquarters is at the Charles L. Sommers Base located outside of Ely near the Canadian border. Four trips, each with a different character, length, and price are offered from May through September. The Charles L. Sommers Base also offers an Okpik Winter Adventure, if you like cold weather. The fee schedule is based on the number of people you bring. For planning purposes, average daily cost per person is about $30. Check the base brochure (produced yearly) for details, schedules, and rates. (Scholarships available; employment opportunities available.)

Philmont Scout Ranch

The BSA's most active base is Philmont, having had more than 500,000 campers and leaders hike its 137,493-acre mountain wilderness. Expeditions are available on a daily basis from mid-June through mid-August. For Philmont treks, you must plan well ahead. One of the most popular Venturing programs is the Cavalcade, which is a trek on horseback. For an opportunity to do the Cavalcade, you must send a card indicating your interest for a drawing held in January for the season the following year. In addition to crew programs, there are several programs available for individuals. Additionally, programs in the nonsummer periods can be arranged. Weekend programs are available from September through mid-November. A Kanik cold-weather adventure is offered in January and February. Summer rates vary. Check the base brochure (produced yearly) for details, schedules, and rates. (Scholarships available; employment opportunities available.)

LEADERSHIP

VISION
COMMUNICATION
ORGANIZATION
SYNERGISM

RESOURCES

*Venturing
Leadership
Skills Course*
No. 34340A

Leadership

Leadership development and the opportunity to lead are probably the most important elements in Venturing. It is hoped you will get an opportunity to lead, either as an elected officer or as an activity manager. An activity manager is responsible for planning and running crew activities such as a weekend outing, the crew open house in September, or even your crew's superactivity. Being a good leader as well as a good follower makes the group much more effective. In addition to the responsibility of leadership within your crew, consider that one day you will be adult leaders. The future needs you to be effective leaders.

Venturing Leadership Skills Course

To assist you, whether you are a crew officer or not, the *Venturing Leadership Skills Course* will help you to become a better leader. This weekend-long course, conducted by your crew Advisors, is required for the Silver Award. The course also is required for the Advisor's Award of Merit. The four sessions included in the course are Vision, Communications, Organization, and Synergism.

In addition to these four key elements of leadership, you also will learn another very important leadership skill called *reflection.* Another word to describe reflection might be "analysis." All good leaders go through this process after completing a challenge or task. It is a way of looking back or reflecting on what went well or what could have gone better or differently. When this step is done, future efforts can be improved.

Vision

A good leader has to know where he or she is going and be able to motivate others to go there too. Vision focuses on the objective while inspiring group members toward that objective.

Communication

Since leaders don't operate alone—they lead others—communication must be effective. Otherwise confusion results. Communication is simply the process by which information is exchanged between individuals. Many of the world's problems are caused by lack of effective communication.

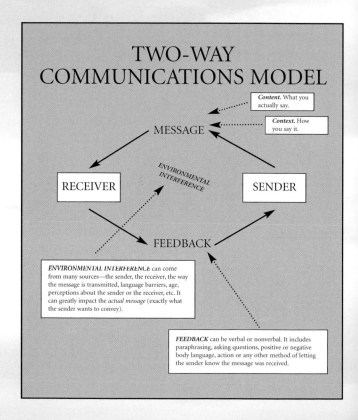

TWO-WAY COMMUNICATIONS MODEL

MESSAGE

Content. What you actually say.

Context. How you say it.

RECEIVER

SENDER

ENVIRONMENTAL INTERFERENCE

FEEDBACK

ENVIRONMENTAL INTERFERENCE can come from many sources—the sender, the receiver, the way the message is transmitted, language barriers, age, perceptions about the sender or the receiver, etc. It can greatly impact the *actual message* (exactly what the sender wants to convey).

FEEDBACK can be verbal or nonverbal. It includes paraphrasing, asking questions, positive or negative body language, action or any other method of letting the sender know the message was received.

Seven Steps of Good Planning

1. Set a broad goal or objective.
2. Decide what form the project/activity will take.
3. Get everyone affected involved.
4. Consider resources available.
5. Develop a step-by-step course of action.
6. Consider alternatives.
7. Follow through to completion.

Organization

Being organized means to develop a structure, to arrange into a coherent functioning whole, and to arrange by systematic planning and united effort. What a mouthful. In today's language, it means "walk the talk." Talking about accomplishing a task or meeting an objective just won't do. You must be organized—this means yourself as well as those you lead. You might have to assign tasks to others working with you, or you might need to break your plan down into steps to accomplish.

Synergism

Synergism is the combined action of two or more people that results in achieving a result even greater than that which each individual is capable of. It is the state in which the whole is more than the sum of the parts.

For example: $1 + 1 = 2\frac{1}{2}$ or even 1,000.

An effective leader recognizes and appreciates that each person is different and that each person sees the world through their eyes, not necessarily as the world really is. An effective leader must be willing to be flexible and sensitive to all situations and adjust leadership styles accordingly.

Your Leadership Opportunities

Even though the Venturing Leadership Skills Course will cover the heavy-duty material previously mentioned, you will have plenty of fun learning it. The sessions are not all lecture style. You will also learn by doing. Along with friends, you will learn the keys to leadership by doing a series of games and challenges. And, of course, always reflecting about what you just experienced.

Once you have learned the key elements to effective leadership, talk with your Advisors and crew officers about opportunities to lead. It takes practice to be a good leader. Do not be afraid to lead or make mistakes. You will improve in time. The success of your crew depends on you, as both a leader and a follower. Remember, synergy!

Advancement Leadership Requirements

Please check the advancement section of this book for details on the leadership requirements for the Gold, Silver, and Quartermaster awards.

Five Styles of Leadership

Telling

Persuading

Consulting

Delegating

Joining

Leadership in the Crew

Responsibilities of Crew Members

It is very important that the youth leaders and the adults assisting your crew communicate the goals of Venturing to your crew's members. **Every member of a crew is responsible for promoting those goals, not only the officers.** Clear communication helps make the individual responsibilities of the crew members more meaningful. The overall goals should be clarified at the beginning of a Venturing program, and care taken that these goals become an integral part of your discussions and meetings.

Members of the crew should

◆ **Communicate their interests throughout the year**

Those planning activities need a clear idea of the interests of the entire crew. Interests may change and develop over the course of the year, so it is important that members talk about their interests on an ongoing basis.

◆ **Suggest ideas for activities**

Each member should think about and share possible ideas for good activities. In addition, each member should listen to the ideas suggested by others. Suggestions often begin simply by brainstorming possibilities. It's important that members feel free to make suggestions without worrying about their views being criticized. When enough suggestions have been made, then and only then is it time to look carefully at the ideas that serve the best interests of the crew.

◆ **Participate regularly in meetings and activities**

If a crew is to become a cohesive group, the group must meet on a regular basis. Being there is an important part of commitment, and commitment is what holds people together and strengthens a group.

◆ **Vote responsibly for the best interests of the crew**

The most important crew decisions are made by a majority vote of the membership. Members should attend meetings and take part in discussions before voting, listen carefully to the different positions on the decisions that must be made, and speak out before the actual voting takes place. Once a vote has been taken, the members should support the decision voted upon.

◆ **Work with the crew officers to achieve the overall and specific goals of the crew**

Electing good officers is important because they take the lead in activity planning and crew business. All members should carefully consider which members would be good in each office, and consider their own abilities for holding office. Once officers are elected, members should do everything they can to support their officers, offer assistance whenever possible, and take a leadership role for an activity within the year's program. Every member is responsible for contributing to the goals of the crew.

◆ **Serve on activity committees**

An activity committee works out the details of the crew program and puts the plan into action. Crew members will be asked to serve as activity chairs or committee members. The success of each activity and the success of the program as a whole depends on members taking their responsibility seriously and doing their best to make each activity meet the interests and needs of the entire crew.

◆ **Share the expenses**

All members are encouraged to give input concerning the crew budget, and the entire membership votes to adopt or not adopt a proposed budget. Once a budget is adopted, all the members are expected to contribute their share, paying dues and working on money-earning projects.

◆ **Seek the help of the Advisor or other adult leaders**

Any member who has a question or is in doubt about what to do in any situation is encouraged to talk with the Advisor of the crew. That is what the Advisor is for—to guide members and to provide support and assistance.

◆ **Recruit new members**

The best people to recruit other young people for a Venturing crew are the members themselves. Person-to-person contact is the most effective method of recruiting new members who can add fresh ideas and enthusiasm to a crew.

Responsibilities of a Venturing Officer

As a Venturing officer, you will be encouraged to take responsibility for many facets of the crew's operations. Some areas of responsibility will be harder for you to master than other areas. But learning to take responsibility for others is part of the maturation process—part of growing up.

Your role as a Venturing officer is

◆ Fostering and developing an environment within your Venturing crew that has a true sense of community, that encourages growth and responsibility to one another

◆ Working in a spirit of partnership with the Advisors of your crew

◆ Developing a program of activities for your crew and helping to carry them out

◆ Upholding the standards and policies of the chartered organization and the Boy Scouts of America

◆ Ensuring that activities are conducted within BSA safety guidelines and requirements

◆ Cultivating the capacity to enjoy life—to have fun and to explore as you lead

In the crew officers' seminar, you will have a good opportunity to discuss these responsibilities and to ask any questions you may have.

Use these responsibilities to evaluate how you are doing throughout the year, not as a judgment of your performance, but as an encouragement to improve. Over time, you will find that you have changed—that your ability to lead has improved.

Position Descriptions for Each Youth Officer

A Venturing crew has at least five officer positions:

◆ President

◆ Administrative vice president

◆ Program vice president

◆ Secretary

◆ Treasurer

You not only should become familiar with the position description for your office, you should also be familiar with the job descriptions of the other officers so that you work effectively as a team.

Crew President

◆ Serves as youth leader of the crew

◆ Implements the crew program in cooperation with officers and members

◆ Works closely with Advisors and other adult leaders in a spirit of partnership

◆ Represents the crew at the Teen Leaders' Council meetings and Teen Leaders'

Council annual program planning conference and is available to report to the chartered organization and crew committee

◆ Assists the crew Advisor in conducting the crew officers' seminar

◆ Appoints youth chairs for special projects and appoints special crew officers

◆ Presents the annual report to the chartered organization at the conclusion of the term of office

◆ Assesses on an ongoing basis whether the responsibilities of the officers are being considered and carried out effectively

◆ Approaches Venturing and encourages others to approach Venturing in a spirit of fun and enjoyment

As the president, you are the primary leader of your crew. You were selected by crew members as the best person to lead and represent them. Being president carries honor and privilege, but it also requires hard work, responsibility, and dedication.

You share the responsibilities of leading your crew with the other elected officers, working together to develop a leadership team. When you delegate specific responsibilities to other officers and members, it is your responsibility, with the support of your Advisor, to encourage and follow up to be sure that their jobs have been carried out. You provide leadership at all crew meetings and activities, and you conduct monthly officers' meetings in consultation with your Advisors. Communication with your Advisors, officers, and crew members is essential.

You also represent your crew's members to the chartered organization and to the BSA council through its Teen Leaders' Council. The Teen Leaders' Council is an association of the crew officers and other teen leaders in the area. You should know your own members' needs and desires so that you can adequately represent your crew at these meetings.

You set an example for members by following the rules and standards of the crew. You may counsel individual crew members who have problems, questions, or concerns. Listen to what they say, and help them find answers that are best for the crew.

With your Advisor, direct the planning of your crew program, and use this manual to plan meetings and activities. The crew president appoints crew members to serve as activity chairs. With your Advisor's help, select members who are suited to the activity and need leadership experience. Coaching and follow-up are necessary to be sure they understand what to do.

Don't hesitate to ask your Advisor for advice and help. That is the Advisor's responsibility—to be your counselor and coach. It is likely that neither of you knows everything about Venturing, but together you can learn how to make your crew succeed. It is important that you work through, not around, your Advisor, who is held responsible by the crew's chartered organization and Venturing for the programs and actions of your crew.

Your duty as crew president is exciting, important, and challenging. You are one person who can really make the difference in how successful your crew is. Read the *Venturing Leader Manual* carefully, and attend BSA council Venturing meetings and conferences to learn from other crew presidents.

Administrative Vice President

◆ Serves as administrative officer of the crew

◆ Assumes the responsibilities of the crew president in his or her absence

◆ Leads the recruiting and admission of new members during the year

◆ Organizes and recognizes the achievements of crew members

◆ Conducts opening and closing ceremonies for special occasions as scheduled

◆ Attends all crew activities

◆ Participates in the council's annual Teen Leaders' Council program planning conference

◆ Approaches Venturing in a spirit of fun, and seeks to reflect this spirit in the recruiting of new members and through recognizing the achievements of crew members

Two key responsibilities characterize your position: (1) leading the recruiting efforts for new crew members, and (2) managing the recognition of members.

First, you provide leadership for the recruiting of new members into your crew by ensuring that prospective members are made aware of your crew and are invited to your crew's open house, and by encouraging members to bring friends to crew meetings. You follow up with any members who seem to be losing interest. Find out why, so that their needs can be addressed in officers' meetings and in the planning of program activities.

Second, you are responsible for recognizing members and making them feel a part of your crew. When prospective members come to your crew's open house or to meetings, it is your responsibility to welcome each one. It is also your job to stage the installation ceremony admitting new members if such a ceremony is a tradition of your crew.

It is your responsibility to recognize the achievements of individual crew members, honoring members who win scholarships, win awards, or gain other achievements in or out of Venturing. You may also conduct opening and closing ceremonies to add color and meaning to crew meetings.

Like every officer, you are responsible for maintaining the crew's code and bylaws.

Program Vice President

◆ Serves as the program officer of the crew and, in that position, arranges the program planning process for the crew

◆ Collects and maintains a crew activity file consisting of the program capability inventory, a list of crew member interests and suggestions for activities, program resources, and an annual activity schedule

◆ Determines the interests of the crew members on an ongoing basis (using Venturing activity interest surveys)

◆ Provides support for the chair and committee for each activity

◆ Maintains an up-to-date calendar of crew meetings and activities

◆ Approaches and encourages others to approach Venturing activities in a spirit of fun and enjoyment

Much of a crew's success depends on the program of activities, and managing the development of a good program is the core of your responsibility. Venturing is based on planning a program that meets the needs and interests of crew members. This is done by asking crew members what they want to see their crew do, and being sure that meetings and activities are adequately evaluated after they take place.

It is your responsibility to maintain an activity file of programs, projects, and trips in which the crew could participate. Base this file of ideas for activities on responses you've collected from the PCI, from Venturing activity interest surveys, and from the activity planners completed by activity chairs. Keep your ears open for ideas from unexpected sources, and ask other crews what they are doing.

You are also responsible for keeping an up-to-date crew schedule and being sure that all the members in your crew know what is happening. You maintain the crew's calendar and should coordinate it with school and community calendars to avoid scheduling conflicts. It might be useful to publish a calendar or newsletter on a regular basis to keep crew members informed.

You help the crew's activity chairs plan and conduct successful activities by sharing ideas from the activity file, discussing possible activities, and coordinating their dates with the crew calendar.

One of the crew's adult associate Advisors is recruited to help you with program responsibilities. Meet as often as possible to share ideas, improve the activity file, support activity chairs, and review the interests of members.

Secretary

◆ Serves as the communications officer and, in that position, manages all communications and publicity for the crew

◆ Maintains crew membership and attendance records

◆ Handles crew correspondence and minutes

◆ Coordinates crew publicity through local media, crew newsletters, and the crew's telephone network

◆ Approaches Venturing in a spirit of fun, and seeks to reflect this spirit in the publicity and communications of the crew

Effective communication is a key ingredient in any organization. As the crew secretary, you are primarily responsible for the communication that needs to be put into writing—correspondence, records, and minutes showing decisions, plans, and publicity. It is up to you to ensure that everyone has the right information.

You keep minutes of officers' meetings and crew meetings, which include group decisions and actions taken by officers. You record the names of those assigned to carry out activities, including all dates, times, locations, and important details. You remind the president and the other officers of agreed-upon decisions that affect them. Most people appreciate a friendly reminder.

You keep membership records for your crew using the Venturing Secretary's Records (see the *Venturing Leader Manual* for more details and forms), which will help you keep accurate registration and attendance information. You supervise all the crew's correspondence, calling the officers' attention to important items and writing letters on behalf of the crew.

You help the program vice president publish a schedule or newsletter for crew members and keep them informed about meeting plans, activities, and last-minute changes. You should organize a telephone network among crew members (see the *Venturing Leader Manual* for more details and forms). You handle all publicity through school or community newspapers, newsletters, radio, television, speakers, bulletin boards, and other media.

Effective communication is an important leadership skill. You have the challenge and the opportunity to use this skill for your crew. An adult member of the crew committee may be assigned to assist you. If you become overwhelmed by the publicity and communications needs of your crew, don't hesitate to enlist the help of other crew members. Sharing your responsibility with others is a part of Venturing. It's a quality of good leadership.

Treasurer

◆ Serves as the financial officer and, in that position, maintains financial records and monitors the crew budget

◆ Collects and disburses crew funds

◆ Communicates with the officers and members on a regular basis to keep them informed about the crew's finances

◆ Approaches Venturing in a spirit of fun, and spreads this spirit in carrying out the treasurer's responsibilities

As crew treasurer, you are responsible for keeping accurate records of the income and expenditures of your crew's funds. Your crew expects an exact accounting of all the money taken in or paid out.

You collect, deposit, and account for all money coming to the crew from dues, money-earning projects, or other sources. If your crew collects dues, you keep accurate records and review them with the other officers at officers' meetings. You make regular reports at crew meetings and officers' meetings of the status of your crew's budget and treasury.

RESOURCES

Venturing
Leader Manual
No. 34655B

Use the Venturing Treasurer's Records (see the *Venturing Leader Manual* for more details and forms) to help you set up a budget by estimating income and expenses based on the crew's activity calendar. Review this budget with crew officers, your Advisor, and the chair for each activity.

You see to it that all expenditures are approved by crew officers and the Advisor before writing any checks. Crew members should approve large amounts. An auditor from the crew committee may be assigned to assist you in setting up bookkeeping procedures, bank accounts, and money-handling methods.

Role of the Activity Chair

The activity chair for an activity is selected by the crew president and Advisor and is responsible for (1) planning, (2) promotion, and (3) staging the activity. For relatively simple activities, the activity chair alone may be sufficient to carry out these three responsibilities.

However, some activities in a crew are more complicated. For these, the activity chair recruits a committee and, depending upon the activity, receives help from the Advisor, crew committee, and consultants.

For example, if the activity is a bowling night, the activity chair probably can organize, promote, and run it alone. However, if the activity is a waterskiing party, then the activity chair might need other Venturers and adults to help with things such as equipment and transportation. Use the PCI to find adults who could serve as consultants, obtain equipment, provide instruction, and supervise safety procedures.

When a committee works with the activity chair to plan an activity, the chair and the committee should go through the seven planning steps together. It is the responsibility of the chair to be sure that the activity planner is filled out and filed with the crew records.

Working With a Consultant

Consultants can be a great asset to an activity. Because these adults have been recruited by your crew committee, you need not hesitate to ask them for help. The activity chair should explain the activity to the consultant who is helping and find out how the consultant's expertise can be helpful for the activity. In addition, the activity chair should review with the consultant what is expected of him or her and what equipment or supplies are needed, if any. After this discussion, the activity chair should follow up with a letter to the consultant, summarizing their discussion, so that there is no misunderstanding. Also thank the consultant after the activity is over.

Remember, though, the adult is there to help, not to chair the committee.

Advisor Award of Merit

One of the unique attributes of the Venturing program is the relationship between Venturers and the crew Advisor. The ability to work effectively with young adults as they themselves plan and run the program is a true test of leadership skills. To recognize those adult crew Advisors who do this well, the Venturing Advisor Award of Merit is offered.

Requirements

1. Be a currently registered Venturing Advisor who has served in that position for at least 18 months.

2. Complete Venturing Fast Start and Venturing Advisor Basic Training.

3. Achieve the Quality Unit Award at least once while serving as crew Advisor.

4. Demonstrate the use of the Venturing Silver Award program.

5. Develop youth leadership by effective use of crew officers.

6. Use the crew officer orientation and program planning process.

7. Have a proven positive relationship with the chartered organization and associated Boy Scout troop and Cub Scout pack, if any.

8. Project a positive image of Venturing in the community.

9. Attract and hold Venturers with crew program and operation.

10. Lead crew in completion of the Venturing Leadership Skills Course.

Nomination Procedure

The crew president in conjunction with the crew officers nominates the Advisor. The nomination is approved by the crew committee chairman.

The nomination is then certified by the unit commissioner and submitted to the council service center.

The nomination is then approved by the Scout executive and council commissioner, who should then forward it to the Venturing Division.

Award

The award is a color certificate, No. 33661, with the recipient's name and a square knot, No. 05001, worn with the Venturing device.

Teen Leaders' Council

The Teen Leaders' Council is a districtwide organization that provides an opportunity for BSA teenage leaders to share information with each other, plan district and council activities and events, get training, and communicate with adult leaders in Cub Scouting, Boy Scouting, and Venturing.

The council can be just for teen leaders of Venturing or it can include older Boy Scout youth leaders (at least 15 years old) and Exploring teen leaders. It is up to the local Boy Scouts of America council to decide whether older Boy Scouts and Explorers are included.

It is suggested that the Teen Leaders' Council meet at the same time and place as the Venturing adult leaders roundtable and that the Venturing adult leaders roundtable be at the same time and place as the Cub Scout and Boy Scout leaders roundtables. This will provide an opportunity for youth to interface with the adult leaders of all the programs that Venturing supports.

Possible program ideas for a Teen Leaders' Council include presentation by the American Red Cross on the courses it offers, presentation by a scuba instructor on how to get scuba certification, presentation by an administrator of a children's hospital about service projects that crews can do, learning a skill youth can teach others, learning how to use a global positioning system, and presentation about Venturing participation in the world jamboree.

Things that the members of the Teen Leaders' Council can share with Cub Scout and Boy Scout adult leaders include names of crew members who have expertise in certain areas, such as navigation, wilderness survival, horsemanship, cave exploring, or various hobbies. Venturers could even volunteer their crew to help a Cub Scout pack with a pinewood derby or a Boy Scout troop with a troop leadership development weekend.

Annual Teen Leaders' Council program planning conference: It is recommended that the Teen Leaders' Councils of all the districts in the BSA council meet together at least once annually to choose and plan councilwide teen activities, such as an Olympic Day, advancement days, weekend activities at camp or other fun sites, service projects, and much more. Districts may also have Teen Leaders' Council program planning conferences.

Venturing Advancement Program

Background and Purpose

One of the strengths of the Venturing program is its ability to meet the interests of all Venturers. Sometimes Venturers like to investigate new, different areas. Variety in a crew always seems to make it more fun to go to meetings and outings. Also, Venturers probably have many interests or would like to have more. Because of that desire, and to provide a pathway to many different experiences, the Venturing awards program is offered.

Advancement has been an important part of the Boy Scouts of America since the issuance of the first 12 merit badges in 1911. In 1950, the Silver Award program was also released as the advancement program for older Boy Scouts. From 1950 through 1966, 18,256 Silver Award medals were earned.

The new Venturing awards program is available to all Venturing youth members of the Boy Scouts of America. Its purpose is to provide a pathway for personal development; encourage Venturers to learn, grow, and serve; and recognize the high level of achievement of Venturers who acquire Venturing skills.

How to Start on the Trail to the Silver Award

First, sit down with your Advisor to make a plan of action on how you will earn the Venturing Silver Award. On many of the requirements you will work on your own, while some you will work on with other Venturers. Many requirements will require contacting and working with a specialty consultant, someone who has extensive knowledge and skill in a particular area.

You will learn a skill from this person, and the specialty consultant will determine your proficiency in that skill. You might find it more convenient to work with several other Venturers at the same time with this specialty consultant. Many requirements involve a **time element,** such as working as a volunteer for three months. Take this into consideration when you are planning. You should probably work on several requirements at the same time, such as serving as a crew leader while working on a Bronze Award requirement.

You can receive **dual credit** for work required in different places. Example: If you get certified in Standard First Aid, you can use this credit toward the first aid requirements for the Silver Award, Ranger Award, and Youth Ministries Bronze Award.

When you have completed a requirement have either an Advisor or a specialty consultant initial and date your track sheet to confirm your completion of that requirement.

When you have completed all Silver Award requirements, ask your Advisor or crew president for a Silver Award review. The review committee will be made up of Venturers and adults. They will determine if you have successfully completed all requirements, and then recommend to your BSA local council that the council, representing the National Court of Honor, present you the highest Venturing award a Venturer can earn—the

Venturing Silver Award.

RESOURCES

National Venturing Awards and Recognition Program (flyer) No. 25-884

Venturing— Scouting's Next Step (poster) No. 25-050

Bronze Award

Introduction

You as an individual Venturer probably have many interests or would like to have more. Because of that desire on your part and to give you a pathway to many different experiences, the Venturing Bronze Award is wide open to you. You can even earn all five Bronze awards. It's up to you!

The Venturing Bronze awards are

◆ Sports

◆ Youth Ministries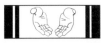

◆ Arts and Hobbies

◆ Outdoor

◆ Sea Scout

Requirement

Earn at least one of the five Venturing Bronze awards.

Procedure

Bronze candidates may have their crew Advisor or a specialty consultant approve or sign off on that completed requirement. Requirements for the Arts and Hobbies, Sports, and Youth Ministries Bronze awards as well as the Gold Award can be found in this book. Complete requirements for the Sea Scout Bronze can be found in the *Sea Scout Manual*. The complete requirements for the Outdoor Bronze Award can be found in the *Ranger Guidebook*. There is no committee review for Venturing Bronze awards.

Bronze Award Device

When you complete the requirements for a particular Bronze Award, you will receive a Bronze Award device, which is a colorful, campaign-style ribbon that may be worn on the Sea Scouting or Venturing uniform above the left shirt pocket. If all five are earned, all five may be worn on the uniform. The Bronze ribbon has an icon representing the area it was earned in superimposed on the ribbon. A certificate is also available.

Earning the whole Sea Scouting Quartermaster or Venturing Ranger Award requires a greater challenge; each has a distinctive award of its own. For more information on these two challenging awards, check out the *Sea Scout Manual* and the *Ranger Guidebook*. You can earn all five Bronze awards as well as the Quartermaster and Ranger awards.

Supply Information

Arts and Hobbies Bronze Award,
    No. 04200B
Outdoor Bronze Award, No. 04200F
Sea Scout Bronze Award, No. 04200E
Sports Bronze Award, No. 04200C
Youth Ministries Bronze Award,
    No. 04200D
Bronze Award Certificate, No. 33666
Ribbon holders:

    One-ribbon holder, No. 04027

    Two-ribbon holder, No. 04028

    Three-ribbon holder, No. 04029

SPORTS BRONZE AWARD REQUIREMENTS

	Date	Advisor's Initials

Do nine of the following:

1. Demonstrate by means of a presentation at a crew meeting, Cub Scout or Boy Scout meeting, or other group meeting that you know first aid for injuries or illnesses that could occur while playing sports, including hypothermia; heatstroke; heat exhaustion; frostbite; dehydration; sunburn; blisters, hyperventilation; bruises; strains; sprains; muscle cramps; broken, chipped, loosened, or knocked-out teeth; bone fractures; nausea; and suspected injuries to the back, neck, and head.   _____ _____

2. Write an essay of at least 500 words that explains sportsmanship and tells why it is important. Give several examples of good sportsmanship in sports. Relate at least one of these to everyday leadership off the sports field.   _____ _____

OR

   Make a presentation to your crew or a Cub Scout or Boy Scout group of at least 30 minutes with the same requirements as for the essay.   _____ _____

3. Take part as a member of an organized team in one of the following sports: baseball, basketball, bowling, cross-country, diving, fencing, field hockey, football, golf, gymnastics, lacrosse, rugby, skating (ice or roller), soccer, softball, swimming, team handball, tennis, track and field, volleyball, water polo, or

	Date	Advisor's Initials

wrestling (or any other recognized sport approved in advance by your Advisor except boxing and karate). _____ _____

4. Organize and manage a sports competition, such as a softball game, between your crew and another crew, between two Cub Scout dens or packs, between two Boy Scout patrols or troops, or between any other youth groups. You must recruit at least two other people to help you manage the competition. _____ _____

5. Make a set of training rules for a sport you pick. Design an exercise plan including selected exercises for this sport. Determine for this sport the appropriate target heart rates and desired training effects. Follow your training plan for at least 90 days, keeping a record showing your improvement. _____ _____

6. Make a tabletop display or give a presentation for your crew, another crew, a Cub Scout or Boy Scout group, or another youth group that explains the attributes of a good team leader and a good team player. Select athletes that exemplify these attributes. _____ _____

7. Make a display or presentation on a selected sport for your crew or another group covering (a) etiquette for your sport, (b) equipment needed, (c) protective equipment needed and why it is needed, (d) history of the sport, and (e) basic rules. _____ _____

8. Research and then, at a crew meeting or other youth group meeting, manage a discussion on drug problems as they relate to athletes. What drugs are banned? What impact do these banned drugs have on the human body and

mind? Where can information about drugs be found? How do some sports organizations fight sports drug abuse? Cover at least the following drugs: stimulants, painkillers, anabolic steroids, beta blockers, diuretics, alcohol, marijuana, and cocaine.

9. Research and then, at a crew meeting or other youth group meeting, manage a discussion on recent training techniques being used by world-class athletes. Compare them to training techniques of 25 and 50 years ago. (This must be different than the discussion in requirement 8.)

10. Study ways of testing athletes for body density. Fat content can be measured by skin-fold calipers, body measurements, and hydrostatic weighing. Then recruit a consultant to assist you as you determine the body density and fat content for your fellow crew members at a crew meeting or special activity.

11. Select a favorite Olympic athlete, a highly respected athlete in your city, or a favorite professional athlete and research his or her life. Make an oral presentation or table-top display for your crew or another youth group.

12. Explain the importance of proper nutrition as it relates to training for athletes. Explain the common eating disorders anorexia and bulimia and why they are harmful to athletes.

(Activities or projects that are more available in your area may be substituted with your Advisor's approval for activities shown above.)

YOUTH MINISTRIES BRONZE AWARD REQUIREMENTS

Date   Advisor's
Initials

Do nine of the following:

1. Earn your denomination's Venturing-age
   religious award.
   See pages 68–69 of this book; pages 12–13
   of *Relationships Resources,* No. 4-400; or the
   Duty to God brochure, No. 5-879.

2. (a) Learn about cultural diversity.

   (b) Make a presentation or tabletop display
   using the information you learned
   in (a) above.

   OR

   (c) Invite someone from a different cultural
   background from yours and the majority
   of your crew's members to give a
   presentation on a subject of his or
   her choosing. Introduce your guest.

   (d) Participate in a discussion about cultural
   diversity with your crew, Sunday school
   class, or other group.

3. (a) Plan and lead a service project such as
   helping to build a Habitat for Humanity
   house, participating in a community cleanup
   project, or taking on a fix-up project
   for a nursing home or nursery.

4. (a) Serve as a volunteer in your church or
   synagogue or another nonprofit
   organization for at least three months.

   (b) Keep a personal journal of your experiences
   each time you worked as a volunteer.

31

	Date	Advisor's Initials

(c) After you have served as a volunteer for at least three months, share your experiences and how you feel about your service with others.   _____ _____

5. Go on a religious retreat or religious trek lasting at least two days.   _____ _____

6. Produce or be a cast member in some type of entertainment production with a religious or ethical theme, such as a play, a puppet show, or concert for a group such as a children's group, retirement home, homeless shelter, or Cub Scout or Boy Scout group.   _____ _____

7. Serve as president, leader, or officer of your Sunday school class or youth group.   _____ _____

8. Complete a Standard First Aid course or higher course or its equivalent.   _____ _____

9. (a) Participate in at least two Ethical Controversies activities as a participant.   _____ _____

(b) Be a facilitator for at least two Ethical Controversies activities for your crew, another crew, your school class, a Boy Scout troop, or another group.   _____ _____

(c) Lead or be a staff member in putting on an Ethics Forum for your crew, your church or synagogue, or your school class.   _____ _____

	Date	Advisor's Initials

10. Serve as a Sunday school teacher or assistant for a children's Sunday school class for at least three months, or as a volunteer for a church/synagogue children's activity such as vacation Bible school.
(This must be different than requirement 4 above.)

11. Meet with your church or synagogue minister/rabbi/leader to find out what he or she does, what they had to do to become your leader, and what they think is the most important element of their job.

(Activities or projects that are more available in your area may be substituted with your Advisor's approval for activities shown above.)

BRONZE

ARTS AND HOBBIES BRONZE AWARDS REQUIREMENT

| | Date | Advisor's Initials |

Do nine of the following:

1. Visit a drafting company that uses state-of-the-art CAD systems and see how the new technology is used. _____ _____

2. (a) Choose a product that you are familiar with. Create an advertising plan for this product, then design an advertising plan layout. _____ _____

   (b) Using your resources, create a clean, attractive tabletop display highlighting your advertising plan for your chosen product. _____ _____

   (c) Show your display at your crew meeting or other public place. _____ _____

3. (a) Learn about backstage support for artistic productions. _____ _____

   (b) Attend a theater production. Then critique the work of the artist in set design, decoration, and costume design. _____ _____

4. (a) Choose a new hobby such as CD, sports card, or stamp collecting; in-line skating; or marksmanship. _____ _____

   (b) Keep a log for at least 90 days of each time you participate in your hobby. _____ _____

   (c) Take pictures and/or keep other memorabilia related to your hobby. _____ _____

   (d) After participating in your new hobby for at least 90 days, make a presentation or tabletop display on what you have learned for your crew, another crew, a Cub Scout or Boy Scout group, or another youth group. _____ _____

	Date	Advisor's Initials

5. (a) Tour a golf course. Talk to the golf pro, caddy, groundskeeper, manager, or other golf course employee about what it takes to operate a golf course. Play at least nine holes of golf. _____ _____

OR

(b) Tour a golf driving range. Talk to the manager or other driving range employee about what it takes to manage a driving range. Hit a bucket of balls. _____ _____

6. (a) Develop a plan to assess the physical skill level of each member of a group such as your crew, a Cub Scout or Boy Scout group, a retirement home, or a church group. _____ _____

(b) Once you have determined your starting point or base, develop a plan with each member of your group to develop a physical training improvement program. _____ _____

(c) Test your group members on a regular basis over a 90-day period to see if there is improvement. _____ _____

(d) Share your results with the group and/or your crew. _____ _____

7. (a) Lead or participate in a crew discussion on the merits of a young person choosing a sports hobby such as golf, jogging, or cycling for a lifetime. Discuss health benefits, opportunity to associate with friends, costs, etc. _____ _____

(b) Ask an adult who is not active in your crew and who has an active sports hobby to join your discussion to get his or her point of view. _____ _____

	Date	Advisor's Initials

8. Visit a hobby store. Talk with the manager about what the most popular hobby is relative to what is purchased and the type and age of people who participate in different hobbies. If they have free literature about beginning hobbies, share it with your crew members. _____ _____

9. Teach disadvantaged or disabled people a sport and organize suitable competitions, or help them develop an appreciation for an art or hobby new to them. _____ _____

10. Organize a hobby meet (a place where people gather to display and share information about their hobbies) for your crew, another crew, a church group, a Cub Scout or Boy Scout group, a retirement home, a group home, or another group. _____ _____

11. Organize a photography contest in your crew, another crew, a church group, a Cub Scout or Boy Scout group, a retirement home, a group home, or another group. Secure prizes and judges. Plan an awards program. _____ _____

	Date	Advisor's Initials

12. Using your artistic ability, volunteer to do the artwork for an activity for your crew, another crew, a Cub Scout or Boy Scout group, a district, or a council. Example: Do the posters and promotional materials for a district Cub Scout day camp.

(Activities or projects that are more available in your area may be substituted with your Advisor's approval for activities shown above.)

OUTDOOR BRONZE AWARD REQUIREMENTS*

For the Outdoor Bronze Award, complete at least four core requirements and at least two electives.

	Date	Advisor's Initials

Do four of the following core requirements:

1. Standard First Aid _____ _____
2. Wilderness Survival _____ _____
3. Communications _____ _____
4. Leave No Trace _____ _____
5. Cooking _____ _____
6. Land Navigation _____ _____
7. Emergency Preparedness _____ _____
8. Conservation _____ _____

Do two of the following elective requirements:

1. Backpacking _____ _____
2. Cave Exploring _____ _____
3. Cycling/Mountain Biking _____ _____
4. Ecology _____ _____
5. Equestrian _____ _____
6. First Aid _____ _____
7. Fishing _____ _____

*Details on these requirements can be found in the *Ranger Guidebook*.

BRONZE

	Date	Advisor's Initials
8. Hunting	_____	_____
9. Lifesaver	_____	_____
10. Mountaineering	_____	_____
11. Outdoor Living History	_____	_____
12. Physical Fitness	_____	_____
13. Plants and Wildlife	_____	_____
14. Project COPE	_____	_____
15. Scuba Certification	_____	_____
16. Shooting Sports	_____	_____
17. Watercraft	_____	_____
18. Winter Sports	_____	_____

SEA SCOUT BRONZE AWARD REQUIREMENTS*

For the Sea Scout Bronze Award, complete the following requirements.

	Date	Advisor's Initials
Ideals		
1. Give explanation	_____	_____
2. History of flag	_____	_____
Active Membership		
3. Seventy-five percent attendance	_____	_____
4. Complete quarterdeck training	_____	_____
5. Recruit new member	_____	_____
Special Skills		
6. Boats	_____	_____
7. Marlinspike seamanship	_____	_____
8. Ground tackle	_____	_____
9. Piloting	_____	_____
10. Communications	_____	_____
11. Time	_____	_____
12. Swimming	_____	_____
13. Cruising	_____	_____
14. Safety	_____	_____
15. Galley	_____	_____
16. Sailing	_____	_____
17. Work	_____	_____

*Details on these requirements can be found in the *Sea Scout Manual.*

	Date	Advisor's Initials

18. Electives. Do any three.

    a. Drill _____ _____

    b. Signaling _____ _____

    c. Compass _____ _____

    d. Yacht racing _____ _____

    e. Sailing _____ _____

    f. Ornamental ropework _____ _____

    g. Engines _____ _____

Gold Award

Introduction

The Gold Award is available to all Venturing members of the Boy Scouts of America.

The purpose of the Gold Award program is to

◆ Recognize achievement by young adults.

◆ Encourage personal growth through exposure to activities related to the following areas: citizenship, leadership, service to others, community/family, outdoor experience, and total fitness.

◆ Offer challenging and stimulating opportunities for young adults to develop and achieve personal goals in leadership, character development, and personal fitness.

◆ Provide a favorable image of Venturing among youth, parents, schools, and communities.

Background

Venturers should have the opportunity to work toward tangible, challenging goals, and to be recognized for their efforts.

The Gold Award program has been developed to recognize a significant accomplishment in a young person's life; it requires outstanding performance in a broad spectrum of activities. The program was developed to challenge and to motivate young people over an extended period of time.

Procedure

Candidates for the Venturing Gold Award must submit a written petition to their crew Advisor, in which they should outline their plans and ambitions for their projects to achieve the award. Advisors are encouraged to have a conference with each candidate to ensure that the Venturer has developed a well-conceived plan, and that he or she has specific goals in mind. After completing all work, a crew review committee including four to six Venturers and Venturing adults will review the candidate's written presentation and interview the candidate to determine if he or she has successfully fulfilled the requirements for the Gold Award.

The program is designed to challenge young men and young women with interests that cover a wide variety of Venturing activities. Several requirements must be met to qualify for the Gold Award; the requirements are listed separately below.

The Gold Award will be presented only to young adults whose personal conduct is in keeping with the principles of the Venturing Oath and the Boy Scouts of America.

Requirements

The Venturing Gold Award program is designed to permit adaptation of certain phases of the program so that all Venturers may work for and achieve the award. In order to offer a challenge to youth, and in the interest of maintaining a standard of qualification, minimum requirements have been established that must be met before the Gold Award can be presented to a Venturer. These requirements are:

1. The candidate must have at least 12 months' **tenure** as an active, registered Venturer before final qualification.

2. The candidate must have been an active member of the Venturing crew, and served in one or a combination of **leadership roles** within the past 12 months (roles may be concurrent) as follows.

For leadership roles within the crew, a candidate might be:

a. A crew officer.

b. A team leaders' council member or committee member.

c. An activities chairman for one of the crew's two-day activities or superactivity.

For leadership roles outside the crew, a candidate might be:

a. An elected youth officer of a religious or school organization.

b. An elected or appointed team leader.

3. The candidate must have **participated** in a district, council, area, region, or national Venturing event.

4. The candidate must, in consultation with the crew Advisor or a member of the crew committee, set and accomplish one personal growth goal related to each of the following areas: citizenship, leadership, service to others, community/family, outdoor experience, and total fitness.

For personal growth, a candidate might

a. Complete a cardiopulmonary resuscitation (CPR) course or an Emergency Medical Technician (EMT) course.

b. Plan and carry out a personal exercise program over a four-month period, i.e., jogging, running, swimming, weight reduction, or physical conditioning.

c. Practice for, and attain, the Presidential Physical Fitness Award.

d. Complete a reading program of the scriptures, classic literature, historical series, etc.

e. Serve for six months as a reading counselor for a child with reading problems.

f. Visit a nursing home, on a regular basis, over a four-month period, to help write letters or to read to patients or provide personalized services.

5. The candidate must plan, prepare for, and lead to completion two or more **crew activity projects** that relate to at least two of the following areas: citizenship, leadership, service to others, community/family, outdoor experience, and total fitness. Suggested crew activity projects are listed separately below.

For crew/ship activities, the action should involve at least five Venturers, and it should require a minimum of four to six months from inception to completion; the project should be approved and the goals of the project set by the crew Advisor and/or a member of the crew committee and the Venturer candidate. Both parties should certify the completion of the

project(s). Activities should be arranged to fit into normal crew programming. Qualifying crew/ship activities include, but are not limited to, the following:

a. Plan and, with the help of at least four other Venturers, carry out a conservation project that is approved by an agency of the federal, state, or local government, such as the National Park Service, the Department of the Interior, the Bureau of Land Management, state division of parks and recreation, city or county parks department, etc.

b. Plan and chair a committee that stages a major social activity involving crew members and their parents, or crew members and their entire families.

c. Plan and carry out a series of crew activities over a four- to six-month period, related to an interest of crew members. Professional or volunteer consultants could be asked to present information regarding their specialty, profession, or occupation.

d. Help organize a new Venturing crew, or revitalize an inactive crew; coordinate activity with BSA local council staff members.

e. Organize a recruitment drive to add members to your own crew or to other crews in the district/council. The drive should last at least one month, and the recruitment plan should include specific activities oriented toward recruiting new members, goals, methods of publicity, etc.

6. The candidate must be able to **recite the Venturing Oath.**

7. The candidate must submit three **letters of recommendation** to the crew Advisor that confirm he or she lives in accordance with the principles of the Venturing Oath. The letters should come from adults outside the crew, such as school or religious leaders, employers, or community leaders.

8. After completing all other requirements, the candidate should prepare evidence of completion of the work and submit it to the crew Advisor. The crew president, in conjunction with

the crew Advisor, should then appoint a review committee of four to six people including Venturers and adults. The committee should review the candidate's **written presentation and interview** the candidate to determine whether that person grew as a result of the pursuit of the Gold Award.

9. Finally, the candidate must have qualified for the Gold Award before his or her **21st birthday.**

Gold Award Device

After many months of determined service and leadership, the Venturing Gold Award should be presented in a setting worthy of the award. Suggested occasions include high school assemblies, religious services, and council Venturing events. The award may be presented more than once. The award is a gold medal featuring the Venturing logo inside a compass dial. The medal is suspended from a white ribbon worn on the left pocket of the Venturing field uniform on special occasions. For daily wear, a white ribbon device similar to the Bronze awards may be worn. It is worn above the left uniform

pocket on the same rack with the Bronze awards. A certificate is also available.

Suggested Qualifying Activities

Because of the designed, flexible nature of the program, crew Advisors and crew committee members are permitted a reasonable degree of latitude in approving activities that serve to meet the qualifying requirements for the Gold Award in the areas of leadership, personal growth, and crew activity projects. Likewise, crew Advisors, crew committee members, and Venturers are encouraged to seek out additional appropriate activities, bearing in mind the purpose of the Gold Award program.

NOTE: The Gold Award is recognized nationally; however, the program is administered and approved, and recognition is made, at the local council level.

Supply Information

Councils (only) may order the Gold Award from the BSA National Distribution Center:

Medal, No. 04187 (for formal wear)

Gold Award Bar (white), No. 04200A

Certificate, No. 33665

Venturing Gold Award Application

Please print or type all information. Give month, day, and year for all dates.

Part I—Personal Data:

Name _____ Nickname _____

Address _____ P.O. Box _____

City _____ State _____ Zip _____

Telephone _____ Birthdate _____

School/College _____ Grade _____

Church or Religious Affiliation _____

Date Entered Venturing _____ Date Bronze earned _____

Part II—Requirements (as they pertain to the requirements for the Gold Award; attach additional sheets as necessary):

A. Tenure: _____ months   Qualified: _____
(Advisor—sign/date)

B. Leadership: _____

_____

_____   Qualified: _____
(Advisor—sign/date)

C. Participation (district, council, area, regional, national events):

_____

_____

_____   Qualified: _____
(Advisor—sign/date)

D. Personal Growth (describe briefly at 1–6 below):

1. _____   4. _____

2. _____   5. _____

3. _____   6. _____

Approved: _____   Completed: _____
     (Advisor/crew committee—sign)   (Venturer—sign/date)

Qualified: _____
          (Advisor—sign/date)

E. Crew/Ship Activities (describe briefly at 1 and 2 below):

1. _____

Approved: _____   Completed: _____
     (Advisor/crew committee—sign)   (Venturer—sign/date)

2. _____

Approved: _____   Completed: _____
     (Advisor/crew committee—sign)   (Venturer—sign/date)

F. Oral Venturing Oath Presentation:

Made before Venturing crew on _____
          (Date)

Completed: _____
          (Venturer—sign/date)

Qualified: _____
          (Advisor—sign/date)

G. Letters of Recommendation/Statements of Venturer's Conduct:

_____ School/Church   _____ Employer/Community Leader

_____ Neighbor/Acquaintance

Qualified: _____
          (Advisor—sign/date)

H. Presentation (orally *and* in writing):

Made before Venturing crew review committee on _____
(Date)

Qualified: _____
(Review committee chairman—sign/date)

I. Qualified before 21st birthday? YES/NO ___ _____
(Advisor—sign/date)

Part III—Certification of Candidate:

Since becoming a candidate for the Gold Award, I have planned, developed, and completed the activities and projects required for qualification for the award. I subscribe to the Venturing Oath, and I consider my conduct to be in keeping with the principles of the Boy Scouts of America.

_____
(Candidate's signature)

Crew No. _____

Chartered organization: _____

Part IV—Endorsement of Crew Advisor/Crew Committee Chairman:

I/we certify that the candidate is well qualified for the Gold Award, that he/she has fulfilled the requirements for the award, and that he/she has my/our complete recommendation for recognition of this significant achievement.

Advisor _____ Date _____

Crew committee chairman _____ Date _____

Part V—Council Certification/Recognition:

Region _____ Area _____ Council _____
                                          (Name)   (Number)

This candidate is a currently registered Venturer. Having completed the requirements for the Gold Award, he/she is to be congratulated for the time, energy, and perseverance required to achieve this recognition. Presentation of the Gold Award is authorized.

Scout executive _____ Date _____

RESOURCES

Gold Award
application,
No. 25-022

Silver Award

Introduction

The Venturing Silver Award is available to all youth Venturing members of the Boy Scouts of America. The purpose of the Venturing Silver Award is to:

- Provide a pathway for personal development.

- Encourage Venturers to learn, grow, and serve.

- Recognize the high level of achievement of Venturers who acquire Venturing skills.

◆ Identify trained and highly motivated Venturers who will be a training, leadership, and program resource for other Venturers, Scouts, organizations, and the community.

◆ Help define Venturing.

Background

Even though your crew's program may be different from another crew's, you share some similarities with other Venturers. First is your age, since all Venturers must be at least 14 years old and not yet 21. Next is your curiosity and desire to learn more about life and the things around you. You probably like exciting, informative programs and activities at your crew meetings. You want to acquire new, usable skills that make you feel like you are really growing in your life. You like a challenge. And, you like to be recognized for your hard work and achievement.

Venturing should be an exciting, advanced-level program where you learn and use advanced skills for your own enjoyment and growth, as well as to benefit others. Life is a series of experiences,

and the Venturing Silver Award is similar. It will lead you on a pathway of exciting life experiences that will guide you to become a skilled Venturing leader.

Earning the Venturing Silver Award will identify you as a Venturer who:

> *has direction in his or her life,*
>
> *knows how to plan and accomplish goals,*
>
> *is skilled,*
>
> *lives the Venturing Oath,*
>
> *is a leader,*
>
> *is willing to serve others, and*
>
> *is one of the proud few to wear the Venturing Silver Award.*

Procedure

Like any high, worthwhile recognition, the Venturing Silver Award will be challenging and will take time to earn. It will take you at least 12 months, but there is no limitation on the maximum amount of time other than you will need to complete all work before your 21st birthday.

Requirements (Overview). These are requirements that all Venturing Silver Award candidates must complete:

1. Earn one Venturing Bronze Award.

2. Earn the Venturing Gold Award, which includes knowing and living the Venturing Oath, service, personal development, and 12 months' tenure.

3. Be proficient in emergency preparedness, including earning Standard First Aid and CPR certification, and knowing and using BSA Safe Swim Defense.

4. Demonstrate leadership, including successfully completing the Venturing Leadership Skills Course.

5. Participate in the Ethics in Action program, including Ethical Controversies activities and an Ethics Forum.

6. Show a crew review committee you have met the requirements for the Venturing Silver Award.

Emergency Preparedness

Introduction

Being prepared has always been one of the key tenets of Scouting. Being prepared continues to be important for today's action-oriented, can-do-anything Venturers. Venturers must be prepared to take care of themselves as well as be ready to serve others when called. When faced with an emergency, people react in various ways. Some people leave, some panic, some do nothing at all, and some respond. Venturers should be prepared to respond!

Requirements

1. **Become certified in Standard First Aid or equivalent course.** If you choose the American Red Cross Standard First Aid version of the course, the curriculum includes how to recognize an emergency and overcome the reluctance to act; how to recognize and care for breathing and cardiac emergencies in adults (training to care for infants and children is optional); and how to identify and care for life-threatening bleeding, sudden illness, and injury. The course is approximately 6½ hours. Your Standard First Aid certification will expire three years from the date of issue. Your CPR certification will expire one year from the date of issue.

If you hold an unexpired certification in this or a higher course, you can receive credit for this requirement. However, you must be currently certified at the time of your Silver Award crew review. You are encouraged to get certified as soon as possible and stay certified. For this requirement you are not required to seek a higher

certification, but you are encouraged to get certifications in higher-level courses such as First Aid—Responding to Emergencies or Emergency Response. You will be even more prepared.

NOTE: If you need help finding an American Red Cross instructor in your area, call your local Red Cross chapter. For literature, call toll-free 1-800-667-2968.

2. **Become certified in CPR.** You can take a stand-alone CPR course or take it as part of another course such as Standard First Aid. Please remember that CPR certification lasts for only one year, at which time you will need a refresher course. Like Standard First Aid, it is good to always be current in your CPR certification. You most likely will get an opportunity to use your skill in saving a life.

3. **Complete the BSA Safe Swim Defense training course.** In this course, you will learn how each of the eight points of the Safe Swim program affects safe crew swimming activities. You will learn that qualified supervision and discipline are the two most important points, upon which the other points rely. You will also learn how to set up a safe swim area. Any BSA aquatics resource person, your crew Advisors, or other council-authorized individual can provide the training course for you. Use Safe Swim Defense, No. 34370A, and Safe Swim Defense Training Outline, No. 19-417.

4. **Either lead or participate in a group swim using BSA Safe Swim Defense.** Swimming can be a great way for you and your crew members to stay fit and to just have fun. To ensure that you and your friends will continue to do just that, always insist you use Safe Swim Defense.

Leadership

Introduction

Leadership is a cornerstone of the Venturing Silver Award. As you work on the Silver Award, you will experience many new things, learn many new skills, and learn to serve others. But to effectively take advantage of all these newly learned skills and experiences, you must know how to effectively lead. It is true that some people are born with some natural leadership ability, but the best leaders develop leadership skills and continue to expand and hone those skills throughout their lives.

We all get the opportunity to be followers and leaders. It takes skill to be a good follower, too, but in this section, you will concentrate on developing leadership skills and implementing those skills as a leader.

Requirements

1. **Successfully complete the Venturing Leadership Skills Course.**

2. **Successfully serve for at least six months in an elected or appointed crew, district, or council leadership position.** Since leadership is a form of service to others, don't be afraid to ask your followers, those you serve, how you are doing. If you don't have an occasional assessment of your progress, you might not improve. Learn to value the opinion of others.

This must be in addition to the leadership requirement in the Venturing Gold Award.

Ethics in Action

Introduction

Another cornerstone of the Venturing Silver Award is learning through experience. While you are working on your Venturing Silver Award requirements, you will have many experiences. You will enjoy experiences that let you interact with your peers, learn decision-making skills, evaluate and reflect so that you can learn from your successes and failures, and discuss conflicting values and form your own value system. Experience can be a powerful learning tool!

Requirements

1. Participate in at least two Ethical Controversies activities from chapter 9 of the *Venturing Leader Manual*. These activities are scenarios that will put you and those who do the activities with you into challenging, problem-solving situations. In a constructive way, these activities will help you develop the following personal skills:

   a. Promoting productive conflict resolution

   b. Polite disagreement

   c. Listening to new ideas

   d. Understanding other people's perspectives

e. Working toward a solution that the group involved will support and implement

2. **Either organize and lead, or help organize and lead, an Ethics Forum for your crew, another crew, school class, or other youth group.** An Ethics Forum is simply another, more formal, way of gathering information about ethics. You will invite two or more adults to form a panel for your crew or group to ask questions about ethics in their personal or professional lives. You can even invite adults related to your crew's specialty; if you are in a sports crew, you could invite a sports doctor, a coach, and a professional athlete. You can even invite guests such as family members and friends to join you. You can even use the information gathered from the Ethics Forum to develop your own Ethical Controversies activities.

Silver Award Review

After completing all requirements, the candidate should prepare evidence of completion of work. It should be submitted to the crew Advisor along with the completed and personally signed Silver Award Progress Record and Application. The crew president, in conjunction with

the crew Advisor, should then appoint a review committee of four to six people including Venturers and adults. The review committee should review the candidate's written documentation and interview the candidate to determine whether the candidate completed all work and grew as a result of the pursuit of the Silver Award. The application is then approved by the crew Advisor and crew committee chairman and submitted to your council service center.

Silver Award Device

The Venturing Silver Award medal features an eagle superimposed over a compass dial. It also has a red, white, and blue background behind the eagle. The medal is worn suspended from a green and white ribbon which is suspended from a silver Venturing bar. A cloth knot and certificate are also available.

Supply Information

Councils (only) may order the Silver Award from the BSA National Distribution Center:

Medal, No. 04186

Square knot, No. 05027

Certificate, No. 33664

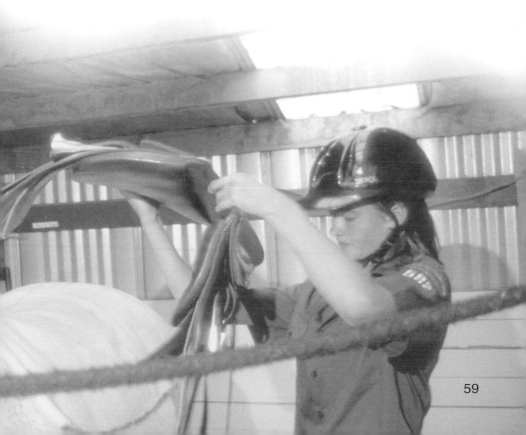

Venturing Silver Award Progress Record and Application

Please print or type all information. Give month, day, and year for all dates.

Part I—Personal Data:

Name _____ Nickname _____

Address _____

City _____ State _____ Zip _____

Home phone _____ Birthday _____

School or college _____ Grade or year in college _____

Church or religious affiliation _____

Date entered Venturing _____

Part II—Requirements:

(Requirements are listed in no particular order)

1. Venturing Bronze Awards (Earn at least one.):

   _____ _____ Sports
   mm/dd/yy Advisor approval

   _____ _____ Youth Ministries
   mm/dd/yy Advisor approval

   _____ _____ Arts and Hobbies
   mm/dd/yy Advisor approval

   _____ _____ Sea Scout (Half of Quartermaster)
   mm/dd/yy Advisor approval

   _____ _____ Outdoor (Half of Ranger)
   mm/dd/yy Advisor approval

2. Emergency Preparedness:

   _____ _____ Completed Standard First Aid or
   mm/dd/yy Advisor approval equivalent course

   _____ _____ Completed CPR certification
   mm/dd/yy Advisor approval

   _____ _____ Completed the BSA Safe Swim Defense
   mm/dd/yy Advisor approval training course

   _____ _____ Led or participated in a group swim using the
   mm/dd/yy Advisor approval BSA Safe Swim Defense

3. Leadership:

   _____ _____ Completed the Venturing Leadership
   mm/dd/yy Advisor approval Skills Course

   _____ _____ Served for at least six months in an elected or
   mm/dd/yy Advisor approval appointed crew, district, or council leadership
   position

4. Ethics in Action:

_____ mm/dd/yy	_____ Advisor approval	Participated in at least two Ethical Controversies
_____ mm/dd/yy	_____ Advisor approval	Organized and led or helped organize and lead an Ethics Forum

5. _____ mm/dd/yy   _____ Advisor approval   Completed Venturing Gold Award

Part III—Personal Certification of Silver Award Candidate:

Since becoming a candidate for the Silver Award, I have personally planned, developed, and completed the activities and projects required for qualification for the award. I subscribe to the Venturing Oath and consider my conduct in keeping with the principles of the Boy Scouts of America. I completed all work on this award before my 21st birthday.

_____
Candidate's signature

Crew No. _____ Chartered organization: _____

Part IV—Endorsement of Crew Advisor/Crew Committee Chairman:

I/we certify that the candidate is well qualified for the Silver Award, that he/she has to our satisfaction fulfilled the requirements for the many facets of the award, and that he/she has our complete recommendation for recognition of this significant achievement.

Advisor _____ Date _____

Crew committee chairman _____ Date _____

Part V—Council Certification/Recognition:

Council _____ Region _____ Area _____
             Name   Number

This Silver Award candidate is a currently registered Venturer. Having completed the requirements for the Silver Award, he/she is to be congratulated for the time, energy, and perseverance required to achieve this recognition. Presentation of the Silver Award is authorized.

Scout executive _____ Date _____

Part VI—Presentation:

The Silver Award was presented to _____
                                                      Name

on _____ in ceremonies at _____.
        Date   Location

Ranger Award

Background and Purpose

High adventure and the outdoors have always been of interest to young Americans as well as an important part of the BSA program. Because of the attraction of high adventure, the Ranger Award is available to Venturing youth members of the Boy Scouts of America.

The purpose of the award is to encourage Venturers to achieve a high level of outdoor skills proficiency; recognize achievement of this high level of outdoor skills proficiency; provide a path for outdoor/high-adventure skills training; and establish Rangers as a highly trained leadership resource for crews, Cub Scouts, Boy Scouts, and the community.

The Ranger Award exemplifies a challenging high-level outdoor/high adventure skills advancement program. Once earned, it will identify a Ranger as an elite outdoorsman who is skilled at a variety of outdoor sports and interests, trained in outdoor safety, and ready to lead or assist others in activities. Rangers can be a great program asset to Cub Scout packs, Boy Scout troops, and others.

Requirements

Ranger candidates must complete eight challenging core requirements:

First Aid	Leave No Trace
Wilderness Survival	Cooking
Emergency Preparedness	Land Navigation
Communications	Conservation

And four of 18 challenging electives

Backpacking	Mountaineering
Cave Exploring	Outdoor Living History
Cycling/Mountain Biking	Physical Fitness
Ecology	Plants and Wildlife
Equestrian	Project COPE
First Aid	Scuba
Fishing	Shooting Sports
Hunting	Watercraft
Lifesaver	Winter Sports

NOTE: Venturers who have received the Outdoor Bronze Award need complete only four more of the core requirements and two more electives to qualify for the Ranger Award.

Procedure

Ranger candidates may work on their own or with other Venturers. A crew may also work together. Candidates may work with outside consultants such as scuba diving instructors. Advisors and consultants must sign a Ranger candidate's record sheet found in the *Ranger Guidebook.* No crew review is required.

Ranger Award Device

After months of experiencing and acquiring skills on a wide variety of outdoor/high-adventure interests and sharing those skills with others, the Ranger will receive a sterling silver medal featuring a powder horn superimposed over a compass dial. The medal is worn suspended from a green and white ribbon attached to a silver Ranger bar. A silver Ranger bar is also available for wear on the field uniform. A certificate is available, too.

Supply Information

Councils (only) may order the Ranger Award from the BSA National Distribution Center:

Medal, No. 04184

Bar, No. 04184A

Certificate,
   No. 33663

RESOURCES

Ranger Guidebook
No. 3128

Earning Boy Scout Advancement

If you are a Venturer who has achieved First Class rank as a Boy Scout in a troop or as a Varsity Scout in a team, you may continue working toward the Star, Life, and Eagle ranks as a Venturer until your 18th birthday.

You must meet the requirements in the *Boy Scout Handbook* and the current *Boy Scout Requirements*. Leadership requirements may be met by serving as president, vice president, secretary, or treasurer in a Venturing crew, or boatswain, boatswain's mate, yeoman, purser, or storekeeper in a Sea Scout ship. The Scoutmaster conference will be conducted by the crew Advisor or ship Skipper. As you meet the requirements for the Star and Life ranks, a board of review is conducted by the crew or ship committee. The Eagle board of review follows the procedures established by your local Boy Scout council.

Venturers working on Boy Scout advancement do not have to be registered in a Boy Scout troop, but may do so at no additional charge. You may pay your yearly membership registration fee in the troop, team, ship, or crew and be a member of the other unit without paying another fee. Example: If you pay to register in your Boy Scout troop, you can also be member of your crew at no additional charge. This is called multiple registration. Just be sure that your membership does not lapse. That is your responsibility.

Venturers who are active in a Boy Scout troop or who are working on Boy Scout advancement may wear Boy Scout rank patches on their Venturing uniform. Venturers who have earned the Boy Scout Eagle award may continue to wear the Eagle patch until their 21st birthday.

Quartermaster Award

Background

The Quartermaster Award, which stands for excellence, goes to the young adult who attains the highest rank in Sea Scouting. The award is a reminder that as a ship needs a rudder, a compass, and a moving force to reach its destination, so an individual must be physically strong, mentally awake, and morally straight to achieve worthwhile goals in life. It represents fulfillment. It results from a young adult's determination to reach goals that he or she has set and achieved in spite of difficulties along the way.

The award is rich in symbolism. The blue ribbon stands for loyalty and country. The compass suggests the importance of carefully chosen direction in life. The wheel reminds us that we are the guide of our own future and that we must persevere with self-discipline. The Scout badge, the emblem of purposeful brotherhood, has challenged and strengthened the lives of more than 40 million men. It shows Sea Scouting as an important part of the Scouting tradition. The anchor reminds us that a truly worthy life must be anchored in duty to God.

This badge of color, beauty, and symbolism, but most of all, of challenge, awaits every Venturer who has the determination to achieve excellence.

Requirements

1. **Ideals.** Must lead a discussion on "Participating Citizenship" and submit a paper on the "World Brotherhood of Scouting."

2. **Membership.** Attend at least 75 percent of ship meetings and activities for 18 months. Present a talk on Sea Scouting and complete a service project.

3. **Special Skills.** Complete the 11 special skills required for Quartermaster, which include:

   a. Boats

   b. Marlinspike Seamanship

   c. Ground Tackle

   d. Piloting

   e. Signaling

   f. Swimming

   g. Cruising

   h. Safety

   i. First Aid

   j. Rules of the Road

   k. Weather

4. **Electives.** Complete four of the following electives: sailing, engine, radio, boat maintenance, electricity, navigation, drill, piloting, rigging, yacht racing crew.

Procedure

Give the application for rank advancement to your Skipper, who will present it to the officers at their monthly meeting. As they review your application, they are primarily concerned with your understanding of the ideals of Sea Scouting as demonstrated by your participation in ship activities. Ordinarily, you will not attend this meeting.

RESOURCES

Sea Scout Manual
No. 33239B

At the quarterdeck meeting, the officers either approve or disapprove your application.

An application for the Quartermaster Award must also be approved by the ship committee and the district or council advancement committee. Following this, the Quartermaster application is forwarded to the National Council.

If your application is not approved, the Skipper returns it to you with an explanation. He or she will help you make corrections so that you can submit it again.

Bridge of Honor

As soon as possible after an application has been reviewed and approved, it should be forwarded through the proper channels. The badge is secured and then presented at an impressive ceremony soon after it has been earned.

The bridge of honor is the ideal occasion for presenting awards. Traditionally, the bridge of honor is held in connection with a social affair. Although this is a good idea, it need not always be done this way.

It is important that each Sea Scout get his or her award as soon as possible. Sometimes there is an unavoidable delay between the date of approval and the bridge of honor. If this happens, the award may be presented informally at a ship meeting and then presented again formally at your next bridge of honor.

Supply Information

The Quartermaster Award medal, No. 04148, is available only through the Venturing Division.

Councils (only) may order these pieces from the BSA National Distribution Center:

Embroidered emblem, No. 04100

Square knot, No. 05009

Religious Emblems Programs Available to Members of the Boy Scouts of America

A Scout is reverent. He is reverent toward God. He is faithful in his religious duties and respects the convictions of others in matters of custom and religion.

To encourage members to grow stronger in their faith, religious groups have developed the following religious emblems programs. The Boy Scouts of America has approved of these programs and allows the emblems to be worn on the official uniform. The various religious groups administer the programs. Check with your local council service center or contact the religious organization directly to obtain the curriculum booklets.

	Cub Scout	Webelos Scout	Boy Scout and Varsity Scout	Venturer[1], Older Boy Scout, Varsity Scout	Adult Recognition
African Methodist Episcopal Church Local council service center or P.R.A.Y., 8520 Mackenzie Road, Suite 3, St. Louis, MO 63123-3413; 800-933-7729; e-mail: info@praypub.org; Web site: www.praypub.org	God and Me (grades 1–3) S, No. 33604; C, No. 33603; M, No. 33606	God and Family S, No. 33597; C, No. 33598; M, No. 33595	God and Church S, No. 33599; C, No. 33600; M, No. 33596	God and Life S, No. 33609; C, No. 33610; M, No. 33605	God and Service Nomination
African Methodist Episcopal Zion Church Local council service center or P.R.A.Y., 8520 Mackenzie Road, Suite 3, St. Louis, MO 63123-3413; 800-933-7729; e-mail: info@praypub.org; Web site: www.praypub.org	God and Me (grades 1–3) S, No. 33604; C, No. 33603; M, No. 33606	God and Family S, No. 33597; C, No. 33598; M, No. 33595	God and Church S, No. 33599; C, No. 33600; M, No. 33596	God and Life S, No. 33609; C, No. 33610; M, No. 33605	God and Service Nomination
Armenian Apostolic Church of America (Western Prelacy) 4401 Russell Ave., Los Angeles, CA 90026; 323-663-8273	None	None	Saint Mesrob	Saint Mesrob	None
Armenian Church of America (Eastern Diocese) D.R.E., Diocese of the Armenian Church of America, 630 Second Ave., New York, NY 10016; 212-686-0710	Saint Gregory	Saint Gregory	Ararat	Ararat	None
Association of Unity Churches P.O. Box 610, Lee's Summit, MO 64063; 816-524-7414	None	God in Me	Light of God Award Nomination	None	Distinguished Youth Service
Baha'i Baha'i Committee on Scouting, Baha'i National Center, Education and Schools Office, 1233 Central Street, Evanston, IL 60201-1611; 847-733-3495	Unity of Mankind	Unity of Mankind	Unity of Mankind	Unity of Mankind	None
Baptist Local council service center or P.R.A.Y., 8520 Mackenzie Road, Suite 3, St. Louis, MO 63123-3413; 800-933-7729; e-mail: info@praypub.org; Web sites: www.praypub.org or www.bsa.net/abs	God and Me (grades 1–3) S, No. 33604; C, No. 33603; M, No. 33606	God and Family S, No. 33597; C, No. 33598; M, No. 33595	God and Church S, No. 33599; C, No. 33600; M, No. 33596	God and Life S, No. 33609; C, No. 33610; M, No. 33605	Good Shepherd Nomination No. 77-062[2]
Buddhist National Buddhist Committee on Scouting, 701 East Thrift Ave., Kingsland, GA 31548-8213; 912-729-6323; fax: 912-729-1699; e-mail: bcascout@eagnet.com	Metta	Metta	Sangha	Sangha	None
Catholic, Eastern Local council service center, diocesan Scout office, or National Catholic Committee on Scouting, 1325 West Walnut Hill Lane, P.O. Box 152079, Irving, TX 75015-2079; 972-580-2114; Web site: www.nccs-bsa.org	Parvuli Dei S, No. 33085 First- and second-graders may earn Light of Christ, No. 33074	Parvuli Dei S, No. 33085	Light Is Life S, No. 16-3011; C, No. 16-106	Pope Pius XII S, No. 33076; C, No. 34733	Saint George Catholic Nomination No. 16-132[2]
Catholic, Roman Local council service center, diocesan Scout office, BSA Supply Division, 800-323-0732; or National Catholic Committee on Scouting, 1325 West Walnut Hill Lane, P.O. Box 152079, Irving, TX 75015-2079; 972-580-2114; Web site: www.nccs-bsa.org	Parvuli Dei S, No. 33085 First- and second-graders may earn Light of Christ S, No. 33074	Parvuli Dei S, No. 33085	Ad Altare Dei S, No. 33094; C, No. 33072	Pope Pius XII S, No. 33076; C, No. 34733	Saint George Roman Catholic Nomination No. 16-132[2]
Christian Church (Disciples of Christ) Local council service center or P.R.A.Y., 8520 Mackenzie Road, Suite 3, St. Louis, MO 63123-3413; 800-933-7729; e-mail: info@praypub.org; Web site: www.praypub.org	God and Me (grades 1–3) S, No. 33604; C, No. 33603; M, No. 33606	God and Family S, No. 33597; C, No. 33598; M, No. 33595	God and Church S, No. 33599; C, No. 33600; M, No. 33596	God and Life S, No. 33609; C, No. 33610; M, No. 33605	God and Service Nomination
Christian Methodist Episcopal Church Local council service center or P.R.A.Y., 8520 Mackenzie Road, Suite 3, St. Louis, MO 63123-3413; 800-933-7729; e-mail: info@praypub.org; Web site: www.praypub.org	God and Me (grades 1–3) S, No. 33604; C, No. 33603; M, No. 33606	God and Family S, No. 33597; C, No. 33598; M, No. 33595	God and Church S, No. 33599; C, No. 33600; M, No. 33596	God and Life S, No. 33609; C, No. 33610; M, No. 33605	God and Service Nomination
Christian Science P.R.A.Y., 8520 Mackenzie Road, Suite 3, St. Louis, MO 63123-3413; 800-933-7729; e-mail: info@praypub.org; Web site: www.praypub.org	God and Country No. 3CSFB	God and Country No. 3CSFB	God and Country No. 3CSCB	God and Country No. 3CSCB	None
Church of Jesus Christ of Latter-day Saints (LDS) LDS Relationships, 36 South State Street, Suite 1175, Salt Lake City, UT 84111-1401; 801-530-0004	None	Faith in God	On My Honor	On My Honor	On My Honor
Churches of Christ Members of Churches of Christ for Scouting, ACU, Box 27938, Abilene, TX 79699-7938; 915-674-3739; e-mail: mccs@bible.acu.edu	Joyful Servant Grades 2–5	Joyful Servant Grades 2–5	Good Servant	Good Servant	Faithful Servant
Eastern Orthodox P.R.A.Y., 8520 Mackenzie Road, Suite 3, St. Louis, MO 63123-3413; 800-933-7729; Web sites: www.praypub.org or www.eocs.org	Saint George No. 3EOMB	Chi Rho No. 3EOFB	Alpha Omega No. 3EOCB	Alpha Omega No. 3EOCB	Prophet Elias Nomination[2]
Episcopal Local council service center or P.R.A.Y., 8520 Mackenzie Road, Suite 3, St. Louis, MO 63123-3413; 800-933-7729; e-mail: info@praypub.org; Web site: www.praypub.org	God and Me (grades 1–3) S, No. 33604; C, No. 33603; M, No. 33606	God and Family S, No. 33597; C, No. 33598; M, No. 33595	God and Church S, No. 33599; C, No. 33600; M, No. 33596	God and Life S, No. 33609; C, No. 33610; M, No. 33605	Saint George Episcopal Nomination
General Church of the New Jerusalem (The New Church) Chairman, Boy Scout Relations Committee, General Church of the New Jerusalem, P.O. Box 277, Bryn Athyn, PA 19009; 215-938-2542; fax: 215-938-2617	Ten Commandments Award	Ten Commandments Award	Open Word Award	Open Word Award	Open Word Award
Hindu North American Hindu Association, 847 East Angela Street, Pleasanton, CA 94566-7511; 925-846-3811 (voice/fax); e-mail: hajratwala@home.com	Dharma	Dharma	Dharma	Dharma	Dharma Saathi

	Cub Scout	Webelos Scout	Boy Scout and Varsity Scout	Venturer¹, Older Boy Scout, Varsity Scout	Adult Recognition
Islamic Mr. Aunali Khalfan, P.O. Box 731516, Elmhurst, NY 11371; 718-779-6505, fax: 718-779-6532	Bismillah	Bismillah	In the Name of God	In the Name of God	Allaho Akber
Jewish Local council service center or P.R.A.Y., 8520 Mackenzie Road, Suite 3, St. Louis, MO 63123-3413; 800-933-7729; e-mail: info@praypub.org; Web sites: www.praypub.org or www.shamash.org/scouts	Aleph S. No. 33185 Tiger Cubs may earn Maccabee S. No. 7165	Aleph S. No. 33185	Ner Tamid S. No. 33181	Etz Chaim S. No. 33186	Shofar Nomination No. 15-102²
Lutheran Local council service center or P.R.A.Y., 8520 Mackenzie Road, Suite 3, St. Louis, MO 63123-3413; 800-933-7729; e-mail: info@praypub.org; Web sites: www.praypub.org or www.tcmnet.com/~lcml/scouting/units/nlas/nlas.html	God and Me (grades 1–3) S. No. 33604; C, No. 33603; M, No. 33606	God and Family S. No. 33597; C, No. 33598; M, No. 33595	God and Church S. No. 33599; C, No. 33600; M, No. 33596	Living Faith S. No. 33637; C, No. 33636	Lamb Nomination; Servant of Youth Nomination
Meher Baba Committee for Meher Baba and Scouting, 912 Ninth Ave. S, North Myrtle Beach, SC 29582; 843-272-9198	Love for God	Love for God	Compassionate Father	Compassionate Father	The Ancient One
Moravian The Moravian Church, Drawer Y, Winston-Salem, NC 27108; 336-722-8126	None	None	God and Country	God and Country	The Order of David Zeisberger
Polish National Catholic Church Mr. Arthur Wyglon, 115 Heather Hill Drive, Buffalo, NY 14224; 716-674-2394	Love of God (Miłosc Boga)	Love of God (Miłosc Boga)	God and Country (Bog I Ojczyzna)	God and Country (Bog I Ojczyzna)	Bishop Thaddeus F. Zielinski
Presbyterian Church (U.S.A.) Local council service center or P.R.A.Y., 8520 Mackenzie Road, Suite 3, St. Louis, MO 63123-3413; 800-933-7729; e-mail: info@praypub.org; Web sites: www.praypub.org or pcusa.org/pcusa/scouters	God and Me (grades 1–3) S. No. 33604; C, No. 33603; M. No. 33606	God and Family S. No. 33597; C, No. 33598; M, No. 33595	God and Church S. No. 33599; C, No. 33600; M, No. 33596	God and Life S. No. 33609; C, No. 33610; M, No. 33605	God and Service Nomination
Protestant and Independent Christian Churches Local council service center or P.R.A.Y., 8520 Mackenzie Road, Suite 3, St. Louis, MO 63123-3413; 800-933-7729; e-mail: info@praypub.org; Web site: www.praypub.org	God and Me (grades 1–3) S. No. 33604; C, No. 33603; M, No. 33606	God and Family S. No. 33597; C, No. 33598; M, No. 33595	God and Church S. No. 33599; C, No. 33600; M, No. 33596	God and Life S. No. 33609; C, No. 33610; M, No. 33605	God and Service Nomination
Religious Society of Friends (Quakers) P.R.A.Y., 8520 Mackenzie Road, Suite 3, St. Louis, MO 63123-3413; 800-933-7729; e-mail: info@praypub.org; Web site: www.praypub.org	That of God No. 3QOFB	That of God No. 3QOFB	Spirit of Truth No. 3QOCB	Spirit of Truth No. 3QOCB	Friends Nomination
Reorganized Church of Jesus Christ of Latter Day Saints (World Community Program Series) Director of Scouting, R.L.D.S., The Auditorium, P.O. Box 1059, Independence, MO 64051; 816-833-1000	None (Use of God and Me—S, No. 33604; C, No. 33603, M, No. 33606—is approved. Contact P.R.A.Y.)	Light of the World	Liahona	Life and World	International Youth Service Award Nomination
The Salvation Army P.O. Box 269, Alexandria, VA 22313; Eastern Territory, 914-620-7427; Central Territory, 847-294-2112; Southern Territory, 404-728-1363; Western Territory, 310-544-6434	God and Me S. No. 33604; C, No. 33603; M, No. 33606	God and Family	God and the Salvation Army	God and Life	Scouter's Award Nomination
United Church of Christ Local council service center or P.R.A.Y., 8520 Mackenzie Road, Suite 3, St. Louis, MO 63123-3413; 800-933-7729; e-mail: info@praypub.org; Web site:	God and Me (grades 1–3) S. No. 33604; C, No. 33603; M, No. 33606	God and Family S. No. 33597; C, No. 33598; M, No. 33595	God and Church S. No. 33599; C, No. 33600; M, No. 33596	God and Life S. No. 33609; C, No. 33610; M, No. 33605	God and Service Nomination
United Methodist Local council service center or P.R.A.Y., 8520 Mackenzie Road, Suite 3, St. Louis, MO 63123-3413; 800-933-7729; e-mail: info@praypub.org; Web sites: www.praypub.org and www.umcscouting.org	God and Me (grades 1–3) S. No. 33604; C, No. 33603; M, No. 33606	God and Family S. No. 33597; C, No. 33598; M, No. 33595	God and Church S. No. 33599; C, No. 33600; M, No. 33596	God and Life S. No. 33609; C, No. 33610; M, No. 33605	God and Service Nomination
Zoroastrian The Zoroastrian Association of Greater New York, c/o Mrs. Villy Gandhi, Corresponding Secretary, The Good Life Program, 704 Harristown Road, Glen Rock, NJ 07452-2334; 201-445-3917; fax: 201-445-3917; e-mail: villy@cybernex.net	None	None	Good Life	Good Life (To age 21)	None

How Do We Get Started on These Programs?

1. Youth members must obtain the specific booklet for their religion.
   - Check with your council store or contact the religious organization directly (see the chart above).
   - Each youth member needs his or her own booklet to document progress.
   - Some religions offer adult manuals for counselors and mentors.

2. Parents must review the program guidelines.
   - Some programs require participants to be official "members" of the religious institution.
   - Age/grade requirements vary from program to program.
   - Each program sets its own guidelines as to who may serve as counselor. Some programs require clergy to serve as counselors; other programs allow parents or other family members to serve as counselors.

3. Families should talk to their religious leaders and show them the booklet before beginning any program.
   - Most programs require that they be completed under the auspices of that religious organization.
   - Many programs require the signature of the local religious leader.

4. The youth member needs to complete the requirements, obtain the proper signatures, and follow the instructions to order the emblem.

- These emblems are not available from your local council store (follow the instructions in your booklet).
- The emblem should be presented in a meaningful ceremony, preferably in the member's religious institution.

Materials with a Boy Scouts of America supply number are available from your local Scout council or from the BSA Supply Division toll-free at 800-323-0732.

**S = student material. C = counselor material.
A = Adult mentor material.**

Notes:

¹The Venturing Youth Ministries Bronze Award is part of the Venturing advancement program. This youth award is not part of the BSA religious emblems programs. For additional information, refer to the *Venturer Handbook*, No. 33493, available from local Scout councils or the BSA Supply Division.

²Also available from Religious Relationships, S226, Boy Scouts of America, P.O. Box 152079, Irving, TX 75015-2079; telephone 972-580-2191.

For more information, contact the religious organizations directly or call your council representative(s).

Venturing Reference Guide

A

activity chair. A Venturer appointed by the crew Advisor and president to chair a crew activity or project.

adult leadership at national high-adventure bases. There are no gender restrictions for adult leaders at national high-adventure bases except that each coed crew must have coed adult Advisors. All adults must be registered leaders. Each expedition, crew, or group must have at least two registered adult Advisors. For Venturing units, both Advisors must be 21 years of age or older. Every crew is required to have a majority of youth participants.

advancement, Boy Scout. Any male Venturer who has achieved the First Class rank as a Boy Scout in a troop or Varsity Scout in a team may continue working toward the Star, Life, and Eagle awards while a Venturer up to his 18th birthday. He must meet the requirements as prescribed in the *Boy Scout Handbook* and the current *Boy Scout Requirements.* Leadership requirements may be met by the Venturer serving as president, vice president, secretary, or treasurer in his crew, or as boatswain, boatswain's mate, yeoman, purser, or storekeeper in his ship. The Scoutmaster conference will be conducted by the Advisor or Skipper. As the Venturer meets the requirements for the Star and Life ranks, a board of review is conducted by the crew or ship committee. The Eagle board of review follows the procedure established by the local council.

advancement, Venturing. The Venturing advancement program is based on achieving proficiency in a variety of skill levels. Advancement includes the Venturing Bronze awards for each of the five Venturing clusters, Venturing Gold Award, Venturing Ranger Award, Venturing Silver Award and the Sea Scouting Quartermaster Award. The Venturing Silver Award is the highest award that can be achieved in Venturing. The Quartermaster Award is the highest award that can be achieved in Sea Scouting.

Any male Venturer who has achieved the First Class rank as a Boy Scout in a troop or Varsity Scout in a team may continue working toward the Star, Life, and Eagle awards while a Venturer to his 18th birthday. He must meet the requirements as prescribed in the official *Boy Scout Handbook* and the current *Boy Scout Advancement Requirements.* He may be registered as a Venturer only.

Advisor, Venturing. The top adult leader of a Venturing crew who is responsible for program, coordination, and the training of the elected youth officers of the crew or ship. The Advisor or Skipper is appointed by the crew or ship committee, approved by the chartered organization, and commissioned, upon approval of the registration, by the Boy Scouts of America. Advisors must be 21 years of age, be citizens or legal residents of the United

States, accept the BSA Declaration of Religious Principle (see "Religious Principle, Declaration of"), and be of high moral character. All adult positions in Venturing are open to men and women.

alcohol. The use of alcoholic beverages by Venturers, leaders, or guests at any Venturing function is prohibited. Adult and elected leaders should be prepared to help crew members understand the serious consequences that can result from the use of alcoholic beverages.

all-terrain vehicles. Motorized recreational cycles with three or four large, soft tires, designed for off-road use on a variety of terrains, are unauthorized and restricted by the BSA.

Alpha Phi Omega (APO). A national service fraternity whose program of leadership, friendship, and service is founded on the principles of Scouting. This coeducational fraternity has chapters at more than 350 colleges and universities. For information contact Alpha Phi Omega National Office, 1100 Waltower Building, Kansas City, MO 64106.

American Youth Hostels. See "Hostels, American Youth."

area. An administrative section of a BSA region containing a number of councils.

associate Advisor. Each crew or ship should have one or more adults, 21 years of age or older, who perform such duties as may be assigned by the Advisor. Associate Advisors must meet the same requirements for commissioning as Advisors and are recommended for commissions by the Advisor and crew committee, subject to their chartered organization and BSA local council approval. Associate Advisors often are assigned administrative and program functions. An associate Advisor in a Sea Scout ship is called a "mate."

aviation. Encompasses orientation flights in powered aircraft, sailplanes, helicopters, and military aircraft; ground school pilot training; all nonflying activities including simulators, building aircraft, tours, seminars, speakers, etc.; and hands-on flying experiences where a Venturer may take control of the aircraft, but the qualified pilot in command of the aircraft, as defined under basic and advanced orientation flights, must be in control of the aircraft at all times. A BSA Flying Permit Application, No. 99-272, approved by the BSA local council is required.

aviation insurance for search and rescue teams. Venturing crews involved in search and rescue activities must not include the use of any type of aircraft for any search and rescue efforts.

awards. Silver Award, Gold Award, Bronze awards, Ranger Award, and Leadership Award.

B

boatswain (pronounced bo'sun). The elected youth leader of a Sea Scout ship equivalent to the president of a Venturing crew.

boxing. An unauthorized and restricted activity by the BSA.

Boy Scout resident camp. Venturers may participate in Boy Scout resident camping if registered and attending with a troop.

However, it is recommended that Venturers attend Venturing camp.

Boys' Life. The magazine for all boys published by the Boy Scouts of America.

Bronze awards. Five Bronze awards are available to Venturers. Bronze awards are offered to recognize Venturers who investigate new and different areas, such as sports, arts and hobbies, youth ministries, outdoors, and Sea Scouting. Venturers may earn all five awards. Achievement of at least one Bronze Award is a requirement for the Gold Award.

C

camping policy. All youth registered in Venturing may participate in crew, district, council, and national Venturing camping activities. Venturers may also participate in national high-adventure programs and world jamborees. Venturers may participate in Boy Scout resident camping if registered and attending with a troop. However, it is recommended that Venturers attend Venturing camp.

cave exploring. The hazardous nature of some caves dictates the need for expert leadership, adequate training, and correct equipment for safe cave exploring. Crews that include spelunking in their program must be under the leadership of a responsible adult who is qualified through training and experience in cave exploring and knows established practices of safety, conservation, and courtesy to cave owners. (See Cave Exploring, No. 19-102.)

chainsaws and mechanical log- splitters. May be authorized for use only by trained individuals using proper protective gear who are at least age 18 in accordance with local laws.

chartered organization. The Boy Scouts of America local council grants an annual charter to community organizations—businesses, industries, labor unions, schools, churches, and other organizations—to operate Venturing crews. These organizations must have purposes compatible with the Boy Scouts of America and be capable of providing adequate adult leadership, program resources, and meeting facilities. The adult Venturing crew leaders must be approved by the chartered organization, be registered with the BSA, and provide sound and moral leadership and the support necessary to provide a successful and wholesome program for young adults.

chartered organization representative. An adult appointed by the head of a chartered organization to coordinate Scouting units within the organization and to represent the organization as a voting member of the BSA local council. The person appointed must be 21 years of age or older and a U.S. citizen, of good character, accept the BSA Declaration of Religious Principle, and be approved by the local council. The chartered organization representative may serve concurrently as crew committee chair or member.

charter presentation. A formal ceremony at which time the charter, leader commissions, and membership certificates are presented to the organization's leaders and members of the crew or ship.

child abuse. The Boy Scouts of America is deeply concerned about the welfare of young adults. The BSA pamphlet, *Child Abuse: Let's Talk About It,* No. 3943, should be used to discuss this issue with parents and other leaders. Suspected cases of child abuse should be reported to the BSA council Scout executive. Child abuse can be physical, mental, sexual, or verbal. It can come from a variety of sources, including other youth, leaders, or parents. The BSA has long advocated that parents should be involved with the activities of their son or daughter, know the crew's adult leaders and other parents, and be involved with the crew's program.

cluster. A grouping of Venturing crews by program interest. National Venturing clusters include arts and hobbies, outdoors, sports, youth ministries, and Sea Scouting.

coed Venturing crews. The membership policy of a Venturing crew is determined by the organization chartering the crew (see "membership requirements"). The organization may determine if its crew is to be coed, all male, or all female (the majority of crews are coed). It is recommended that coed crews have male and female adult leaders.

coed overnight activities. All Venturing activities shall conform to the ideals and purposes of the Boy Scouts of America. To ensure that all coed overnight activities for Venturers and invited guests at crew, district, council, regional, or national levels meet proper moral standards, the national Venturing Committee has established the following policy:

1. The crew Advisor (or Skipper) or council Scout executive must give careful consideration to the number of adults necessary to provide appropriate leadership for both male and female participants. The number of adult leaders required by the hosting facility or organization (such as a BSA national high-adventure base) must be provided.

2. Adult leaders must be 21 years of age or older and be approved by the crew Advisor or Skipper (on behalf of the chartered organization) or by the council Scout executive.

3. Separate housing must be provided for both male and female participants.

4. An adult male leader must be housed with and be responsible for the male participants. An adult female leader must be housed with and be responsible for the female participants.

5. Written parent or guardian approval is required for each Venturer or guest under 21 years of age.

See "leadership policy for all trips and outings."

committee, crew. A group of adult men and women recruited by the chartered organization, through its chartered organization representative, to organize and support the program and leadership of the organization's crew. One person is elected or appointed to serve as chair. The crew committee is responsible for managing the crew's program capability inventory and for recruiting the crew Advisor and associate Advisors. All committee members must be 21 years of age or older, of good character, and U.S. citizens or legal residents; accept the BSA Declaration of Religious Principle; and be approved for a certificate of membership by their BSA local council. A minimum of three persons is required to form a crew committee, one serving as chair.

Conservation Good Turn Certificate. The conservation Good Turn is an opportunity for Venturing crews to join with conservation or environmental organizations (federal, state, local, or private) to carry out a conservation Good Turn in their home communities. (Application, No. 21-386.)

consultant. A person who has special skills, equipment, facilities, or contacts in an interest area related to the crew program.

council. An incorporated and BSA-chartered body of representatives (chartered organization representatives and members at large) from organizations operating packs, troops, teams, and crews. The more than 300 local councils are responsible for the administration of BSA programs in a designated geographic territory.

council service center. The business center for the BSA local council's administration of Scouting.

crew code and bylaws. A set of bylaws adopted by the members of a crew or ship to guide their officers and program. The Venturing Code is included as a preamble.

crew committee. See "committee, crew."

crew officers' seminar. An annual planning and training program conducted by the crew Advisor for newly elected youth officers.

crew, Venturing. Youth members and adult leaders who conduct the Venturing program within an organization chartered by the BSA.

cross-country flights. Noncommercial flights with the sole purpose of getting from point A to point B are unauthorized and restricted by the BSA.

cruise release form. A parental release form may be required by the U.S. Navy and Coast Guard for Venturers participating in military cruises. Samples of these forms are available from BSA local council service centers.

D

disabled persons, mentally and physically. All Venturing crews are encouraged to involve persons with disabilities as members. Chartered organizations using Venturing determine, with the approval of appropriate medical authorities, whether a youth member is qualified to register beyond the normal Venturer registration age limit of 21. The Venturing Advisor/Skipper's signature on the Venturer application or the unit's charter renewal application certifies the approval of the chartered organization.

district. A geographic administrative entity of a council.

district committee. A group of volunteer adults responsible for carrying out the BSA program within a geographic district of a council.

district executive (DE). A professional who works under the direction of the Scout executive and is responsible for the administration of the district.

drivers, youth. Venturers who have a valid driver's license (not a learner's permit or equivalent) are permitted to drive themselves and others in a Venturing activity. For BSA local and national tour permits, Venturer drivers must be 16 years of age, have six months' driving experience, no accidents or violations, and have parental permission for drivers and riders.

drug abuse. The illegal use or possession of drugs or hallucinogens by Venturers, adults, or guests is prohibited at any Venturing function.

E

Eagle Award. The highest advancement rank for Boy Scouts.

emblems. Venturing crews are encouraged to design their own identifying emblems. A crew emblem is not limited in size, but if worn on the sleeve of an official BSA uniform shirt or jacket, it may not be more than 3 inches in diameter and is worn 2 inches below the shoulder seam on the right sleeve. Crew emblem designs should be approved by the BSA local council before they are ordered.

emergency service. All Venturing crews are encouraged to include emergency preparedness training in their program.

ethical controversies. A collection of prepared ethical controversies located. (See *Venturing Leader Manual,* No. 34655B.)

ethics forum. One or more persons who work in the special-interest area of the crew are invited to speak to the crew about ethical issues in the field. Crew members can use the information gathered to develop their own special-interest ethical controversies. See "ethical controversies."

Ethics in Action. In the Boy Scouts of America program, the belief in experiential learning and the values and ethical principles that this kind of learning seeks to promote are referred to as Ethics in Action.

executive board, council. A group of adults elected by the chartered organization representatives and members at large of a local council to be responsible for the ongoing administration and extension of the program of the BSA.

experimental class aircraft flying. Venturers may not participate in experimental class aircraft flying. This is an unauthorized and restricted activity by the BSA.

F

Fifty-Miler Award. A recognition given to members of a crew who make a wilderness hike, canoe, or rowboat trip of not less than 50 consecutive miles in no less than five days and complete a service project on the way.

firearms. The Boy Scouts of America encourages the safe and proper use of rifles, shotguns, muzzle-loaders, and air rifles in outdoor sports. Shooting on BSA camp ranges and in cooperation with other national associations with similar purposes adds to greater knowledge of the safe and proper use of firearms. All training and shooting must be supervised by an NRA-certified instructor or a certified instructor of a local, state, or federal agency. Use of handguns is limited to Venturers, who must complete a basic handgun marksmanship safety course prior to range firing.

fireworks. The use and handling of fireworks can be dangerous and is classified by most safety and fire prevention experts as a hazardous activity. It is the policy of the Boy Scouts of America to prohibit the securing, use, and display of fireworks in conjunction with BSA programs and activities. Further, local councils may not authorize any group acting for or on behalf of its members, units, or districts to sell fireworks as a fund-raising or money-earning activity. This policy does not preclude having a fireworks display conducted under the auspices of a certified and/or licensed fireworks control expert.

flight release form. See "flying policy."

Florida National High Adventure Sea Base. Provides aquatics adventure programs, including canoeing, sailing, scuba diving, and exploring the reefs of the Florida Keys and the Bahamas, for Venturing crews. Contact Florida National High Adventure Sea Base, P.O. Box 1906, Islamorada, FL 33036-1906; phone 305-664-4173.

flying policy. A BSA Flying Permit Application, No. 99-272, approved by the BSA local council, and Parent/ Guardian Consent Form for BSA Aviation Flights, No. 99-273, are required for any activity involving Venturers riding in aircraft other than commercial flights. Venturers may not participate in cross-country flights, experimental class aircraft flying, flying aircraft as part of a search and rescue

mission, hang-glider flying, hot-air ballooning, pilot rating certification in powered and nonpowered aircraft, sport parachuting, or ultralight flying. Councils or units may not own aircraft.

football. Participation on varsity football teams or interscholastic or club football training or competition is not approved as a Venturing activity.

fraternization policy. The Boy Scouts of America does not condone and will not permit fraternization between Venturers and adult leaders or other affiliated adults. This policy applies to all youth members regardless of local or state laws related to age of consent. Fraternization is not morally appropriate, nor in keeping with the relationship between youth members and adult leaders prescribed in the programs of the Boy Scouts of America.

Friends of Scouting (FOS). An annual opportunity for parents and interested people in the community to provide financial support to their local council.

G

Gold Award. The Gold Award is available to Venturers. The Gold Award is designed to recognize significant accomplishment in a Venturer's life as he or she has proven outstanding performance in at broad spectrum of activities. Achievement of the Gold Award is a requirement for the Silver Award.

Guide to Safe Scouting, **No. 34416B.** Pamphlet designed to prepare adult leaders to conduct Venturing activities in a safe and prudent manner; the policies and guidelines in it have been established because of the real need to protect members from known hazards identified through years of experience in the BSA. A free guide is available through your BSA local council service center.

H

handguns. Handgun use in the BSA is limited to Venturing only. All training and shooting activities must be under the supervision of an NRA-certified instructor or the firearms instructor recognized by a local, state, or federal agency.

hand salute/hand sign. Should a Venturing adult or youth in uniform find themselves in a position where a hand salute is appropriate, it is recommended that Venturers and adult leaders use a full-hand salute.

hang gliding. See "parachuting or hang gliding."

hazardous activities. Crew or ship programs should include proper safety and fitness training prior to involvement in activities such as rifle shooting, rock climbing, waterskiing, etc. Venturers should not be involved in projects or activities with potential hazards without proper training, equipment, knowledge of safety procedures, and supervision of qualified adults. See "unauthorized activities."

Heroism Award. (Formerly "Certificate for Heroism.") A lifesaving award presented by the BSA National Court of Honor to a registered Venturer or leader who has saved a life at some risk to his or her own. (Contact BSA local council service center.)

high-adventure bases (national, BSA). See individual listings for Florida National High Adventure Sea Base, Northern Tier National High Adventure Programs, and Philmont Scout Ranch.

Historic Trails Award. Available to Venturing crews planning and conducting historic service projects or activities in cooperation with a local historic society. (Contact BSA local council service center.)

Honor Medal. A lifesaving award presented by the BSA National Court of Honor to a registered Venturer or leader who has demonstrated unusual heroism in saving or attempting to save a life at extreme personal risk. (Contact BSA local council service center.)

Hornaday Award. The William T. Hornaday Award is available to recognize Venturers and/or crews/ships for distinguished service in conservation. (Application, No. 21-107.)

Hostels, American Youth. In addition to the many resources available to traveling Venturers and Scouts, hostels offer another inexpensive housing alternative. Contact an American Youth Hostel Council near you or the organization's national headquarters in Washington, D.C. BSA local councils can take advantage of an offer for a free nonprofit membership by writing to American Youth Hostels, Dept. PE/NEA, P.O. Box 37613, Washington, DC 20013-7613; phone 202-783-6161.

hot-air ballooning. An unauthorized and restricted activity by the BSA.

I

identification. All crews and ships are encouraged to adopt some form of uniform or clothing item that identifies their members as Venturers. Jackets, T-shirts, and other items can be considered. (See "uniforms and insignia (BSA).")

initiative games. Fun, cooperative, challenging games in which the group is confronted with a specific problem to solve.

insurance. The Boy Scouts of America has a program of general liability insurance that covers most liability exposures of Venturing functions and activities. This is a legal liability policy and does not provide medical payments or accident insurance, which pays medical expenses regardless of fault. Accident insurance is available through your BSA local council. The liability policy covers the BSA local council (including crews or ships), the National Council, all Scouting officials, employees, chartered organizations, donors and volunteer workers, young-adult leaders, and certificate holders by specific endorsement. The insured parties are covered for sums which they shall become legally obligated to pay as damages to third parties because of bodily injury or property damage caused by an occurrence arising out of or in the course of Venturing functions and activities. It is excess over other valid and collectible insurance carried by volunteers. Coverage is primary for chartered organizations.

J

judo. See "karate and boxing."

K

karate and boxing. Boxing, karate, and other related martial arts are not approved activities for Venturers. Judo is approved as an activity under the supervision of a qualified instructor.

L

Leadership Award. Available to youth and adult volunteers registered and involved in Venturing. The Venturing Leadership Award is presented by councils, areas/regions, and the BSA National Council to Venturers and adult volunteers who have made exceptional contributions to Venturing and who exemplify the Venturing Code and Oath. Refer to Leadership Award guidelines for annual council, areas/regions, and National Council quota restrictions.

leadership policy for all trips and outings. It is the policy of the Boy Scouts of America that trips and outings may never be led by only one adult. At least two adult leaders, both of whom must be at least 21 years of age, are required for all trips or outings. It is the responsibility of the chartered organization of any Venturing crew/ ship to inform the committees and leadership of the unit that sufficient adult leadership be provided on all trips and outings. (Coed overnight activities require male and female adult leaders. See "coed overnight activities.")

Lifeguard, BSA. Certification available through the BSA for persons qualified to supervise swimming and other aquatics activities. (Contact BSA local council for details.)

M

mate. The Sea Scouts, BSA equivalent of an associate Advisor.

Medal of Merit. May be awarded by the National Court of Honor to a registered Venturer or leader for meritorious action of an exceptional character, not necessarily involving risk to life. (Contact BSA local council service center.)

medical examinations. All Venturers and adult leaders should have medical examinations by their personal physicians before participating in vigorous activities. Venturing Advisors should be aware of any medical restrictions or conditions of crew members that might endanger them during activities or trips. A health history of each member should be requested and updated annually, especially by crews planning strenuous activities.

membership policy. It is the Boy Scouts of America's official position that its youth and adult membership (in all categories and program phases) shall be open to all without regard to race or ethnic background. A charter will not be granted by the Boy Scouts of America to a group that establishes a rule or custom preventing any youth or adult from membership in its Cub Scout, Boy Scout, Varsity Scout, or Venturing unit because of race or ethnic background.

membership requirements. Venturing is for young men and women who have completed the eighth grade and are 14 years of age, or are 15 or older but have not yet reached their 21st birthday. They must pay an annual registration fee, accept the obligation to observe the Venturing Oath and Code, and attend regular meetings of the crew or ship. Membership in a crew or ship requires the approval of the Advisor or Skipper within the policies of the BSA. Venturers registered in a crew or ship before their 21st birthday may continue as members after their 21st birthday until the crew or ship recharters or until they reach their 22nd birthday.

Mile Swim, BSA. A recognition available for Venturers who follow a program of preliminary conditioning and swim a continuous mile under the supervision of a qualified swim coach or instructor.

military policy. Military programs and activities involving Venturers must be conducted under the direction of an official branch or representative of the U.S. armed services or a community organization, such as the American Legion, Veterans of Foreign Wars, etc., whose goals are compatible with the BSA. Crews or ships wearing military-style uniforms must be clearly identified as Venturers and should not be mistaken for military personnel. Improper or illegal paramilitary or guerrilla-type activities are not permitted for Venturers.

military surplus. The BSA is eligible to receive some items declared surplus by military and federal agencies. These items are loaned in perpetuity to BSA local councils, which must retain ownership.

money-earning projects. Crews or ships planning money-earning projects must complete, in advance, a Unit Money-Earning Application, No. 34427, which may be secured from and must be approved by their BSA council. The proposed project must be consistent with the purposes and policies of the Boy Scouts of America as follows:

1. Crew committee and chartered organization approval is required.

2. The projects must not involve any form of gambling and must comply with local laws and permits.

3. Purchasers must receive fair value from the project, service, or function.

4. The project should not compete unfairly with local businesses or individuals needing work.

5. The project must protect the name of Venturing and the Boy Scouts of America, preventing any misuse or desire for endorsement by promoters.

6. Any contracts, orders, or legal agreements must be signed by crew leaders without reference to the Boy Scouts of America and in no way binding to the local councils or National Council of the Boy Scouts of America.

7. A crew or ship may not solicit public donations for its treasury.

motorized speed events and demolition derbies. Motorized speed events with potential hazard for participants, including motorcycle, boat, drag racing, demolition derby, and related events, are unauthorized and restricted by the BSA.

N

National Council. The corporate membership of the Boy Scouts of America is made up of local council representatives, members at large, and honorary members. This group elects officers and an executive board, which establishes policies, develops programs, and grants charters to local councils.

national office (BSA). The national administrative offices of the Boy Scouts of America are located at Boy Scouts of America, 1325 West Walnut Hill Lane, P.O. Box 152079, Irving, TX 75015-2079; phone 972-580-2000.

Northern Tier National High Adventure Programs. Various backpacking, canoeing, and winter camping activities available in Wisconsin, Minnesota, and Canada. Contact Northern Tier National High Adventure Programs, P.O. Box 509, Ely, MN 55731-0509; phone 218-365-4811.

O

open house. A special meeting held by each crew, usually in the fall, to recruit new members.

Order of the Arrow. A Boy Scout honor camper organization. Order of the Arrow youth membership candidate elections will be authorized to be conducted in Boy Scout troops/Varsity teams at the discretion of the lodge and under the direction of Arrowmen serving as members of a lodge unit election team. Further information is available from BSA local council service centers.

ownership of vehicles, boats, facilities, or property. Legal titles of ownership of vehicles, boats, airplanes, facilities, or properties must be held by individuals or incorporated groups in most states. Because Venturing crews or ships do not qualify as either, such titles or deeds should be held by the chartered organization or a nonprofit corporation organized by the adult leaders and/or parents of a crew or ship with the approval of the local council.

P

parachuting or hang gliding. The use of sport parachutes, hang gliders, ultralights, or similar devices is not approved as a Venturing activity.

parents' night. An open house conducted by the crew for parents. Its purpose is to inform and involve parents in crew and council activities.

passenger for hire. Under the Passenger Vessel Safety Act of 1993 (mandatory June 1994), a "passenger for hire" is defined as someone who has contributed "consideration" to the owner, operator, or agent of the vessel as a condition of being taken out on the boat. In such cases, the skipper must have a Coast Guard operator's license. A bareboat charter vessel carrying more than 12 people must now be inspected by the Coast Guard. A vessel of less than 100 gross tons can carry up to six passengers for hire and does not need to be inspected. It is called an "uninspected small passenger vessel."

Philmont Scout Ranch. Camping and hiking programs for Venturing crews in 137,000 acres of rugged northern New Mexico. Includes a center for volunteer and professional training. Contact Philmont Scout Ranch, Cimarron, NM 87714; phone 503-376-2281.

pilot training/rating certification in powered and nonpowered aircraft. The BSA is not a pilot certification agency. Numerous flight schools are available to qualified Venturers or Scouts who desire to become pilots. Scouts, Venturers, and leaders who choose to become pilot-certified do so as private individuals, not as members of the BSA.

political involvement. The crew or ship program should include activities that provide understanding of America's government and political process. Venturers may not be involved in any activity that might imply BSA endorsement of a political candidate or issue.

president, Venturing crew. A Venturer elected as the top youth leader of a crew.

program capability inventory (PCI). An inventory of the program potential of selected adults connected with a Venturing crew, its chartered organization, and the community.

purpose of Venturing. The purpose of Venturing is the same as that of the Boy Scouts of America: character development, citizenship training, and fitness.

Q

Quality Unit Award. Presented annually by councils to crews or ships for achievement in membership growth, quality program, and leader training. (Contact BSA local council for details.)

Quartermaster. The highest rank in Sea Scouting. (*Sea Scout Manual*, No. 33239B.)

R

racing. Motorized speed events with potential hazard for participants such as motorcycle, boat, or car racing, drag racing, demolition derbies, or related events are not approved as Venturing activities.

Ranger Award. The Venturing Ranger Award is available to all Venturers. The purpose of the award is to encourage Venturers to achieve high levels of outdoor skills proficiency and to provide a pathway for outdoor/high adventure skills training. Once earned, the Ranger Award will identify a Venturer as an elite outdoorsman who is skilled at a variety of outdoor sports and interest, is trained in outdoor safety, and is ready to assist others in activities.

rechartering and registration. Organizations using the BSA program must renew their crew charter each year. Each crew member and adult leader also must register each year. New adults and Venturers can register during the year by paying a pro-rated fee until the crew's charter expiration date. Membership application forms are available from the council service center.

reflection. Looking back at recent experiences to understand what happened, and using this understanding in looking forward to the next action and new experiences. We facilitate reflection by asking questions that cause people to think. A good way to practice reflection is to use it with initiative or cooperative games.

region. The BSA is divided into four geographical administrative entities, the Northeast Region, Southern Region, Central Region, and Western Region.

religious emblems. Various religious organizations have designed requirements and procedures for Venturers to earn a religious emblem of their faith. (Contact BSA local council for details.)

Religious Principle, Declaration of, (BSA). The Boy Scouts of America maintains that no person can grow into the best kind of citizen without recognizing an obligation to God and, therefore, acknowledges the religious element in development of youth members, but it is absolutely nonsectarian in its attitude toward that religious development. Its policy is that the organization or institution with which youth members are connected shall give definite attention to their religious life. Only adults willing to subscribe to this declaration of principle and the Bylaws of the Boy Scouts of America shall be entitled to certificates of leadership.

rodeo. Participation in rodeo events is not approved as a venturing activity.

S

safe boating/sailing guidelines. Guidelines and standards that apply to the operation of boating and sailing activities at the unit, district, and council level. BSA-owned boats 30 feet and under are required to have a courtesy marine inspection annually; leaders are required to have completed a basic boating safety course administered by a certified organization or agency. BSA-owned boats over 30 feet are required the same as above plus a condition survey every four years from a recognized or certified marine surveyor. Rowboats, canoes, open-cockpit sailboats, and small vessels propelled solely by oars or paddles are exempt and will comply to BSA Safety Afloat standards. BSA-owned boats are no longer considered passenger vessels and are not required to have a Coast Guard operator's license or certificate of inspection. In such cases where BSA vessels are engaged in a passenger-for-hire situation, the skipper must have a Coast Guard operator's license. See "passenger for hire."

Safe Swim Defense. A plan to help crew leaders plan safe swimming that includes: (1) qualified supervision, (2) physical fitness, (3) safe swimming area, (4) lifeguards, (5) lookout, (6) ability groups, (7) buddy system, and (8) good discipline. (*Safe Swim Defense,* No. 34370A.)

Safety Afloat. The guidelines to help crew leaders plan safe boat, canoe, or raft trips are: (1) qualified supervision, (2) physical fitness, (3) swimming ability, (4) personal flotation equipment, (5) buddy system, (6) skill proficiency, (7) planning, (8) equipment, and (9) discipline. (*Safety Afloat,* No. 34368B)

Scout executive (council executive). The top professional staff leader of a local council.

Sea Scouting. The traditional Sea Scouting program offers an advancement program and awards related to seamanship as outlined in the *Sea Scout Manual,* No. 33239B.

search and rescue aircraft flying. Venturers may not fly in any type of aircraft as part of a search and rescue mission. This is an unauthorized and restricted activity by the BSA.

secretary (crew). A Venturer elected to handle minutes, records, and correspondence for the crew. (See Secretary's Records in the Appendix of the *Venturing Leader Manual,* No. 34655B.)

ship, Sea Scout. Unit that conducts Sea Scouting for the chartered organization, equivalent to a Venturing crew.

Silver Award. The Silver Award is available to all Venturers. Its purpose is to provide a pathway for personal development; encourage Venturers to learn, grow and serve; and recognize the high level of achievement of Venturers who acquire Venturing skills. Candidates must first achieve at least one Bronze Award and the Venturing Gold Award.

skin and scuba diving. Scuba diving instruction, with breathing tanks, is approved only for Venturers at least 14 years of age and only under the supervision of a certified instructor using YMCA (Young Men's Christian Association), NAUI (National Association of Underwater Instructors), PADI (Professional Association of Diving Instructors), NASDA (National Association of Skin Diving Schools), or SSI (Scuba Schools International) standards and courses of instruction. Group dive sessions shall be restricted to certified scuba divers at least 14 years of age under the supervision of a certified dive master, assistant instructor, or instructor certified by PADI, NAUI, NASDA, or SSI. Student divers must be under the supervision of an instructor certified by the YMCA, PADI, NAUI, NASDA, or SSI.

Skipper. The adult leader of a Sea Scout ship equivalent to a crew Advisor.

smoking. Adult leaders should support the attitude that young adults are better off without tobacco and should not allow the use of tobacco products at any BSA activity involving youth participants.

Snorkeling, BSA. A recognition available for Venturers who follow a program using masks and fins, and snorkel under the supervision of a qualified instructor. (Application, No. 19-176.)

sponsor. See "chartered organization."

superactivity. A major annual activity, trip, or project of a Venturing crew requiring long-range planning and extensive preparation. Generally the highlight of the crew's program year.

T

Teen Leaders' Council (TLC). The Teen Leaders' Council is a council- or districtwide group of Venturing youth officers. With council approval and under the direction of an adult adviser, the Teen Leaders' Council plans district- and /or councilwide Venturing activities.

tour permit. A BSA permit designed to help crews and ships plan safe, healthful, and enjoyable trips by following recommended travel procedures. A local tour permit, No. 34426B, is filed with the council for a trip of less than 500 miles. A national tour permit, No. 4419B, is filed with the region

through the council for a trip of 500 miles or more, or a trip into foreign countries. These permits apply to travel by automobile, boat, plane, bus, or other transportation. Proper adult supervision, safety procedures, proper equipment, licensed public carriers, sufficient liability insurance, parental approval, and other safeguards are required. Safety belts must be provided for and be used by each passenger and driver. No persons may be transported in the beds of trucks, trailers, or campers. (Contact BSA local council for details.)

training awards (BSA). Recognition is available for adult Venturing leaders for training, tenure, and performance. A Venturing Key is available for crew Advisors. The Venturing Training Award is available for other adult leaders.

travel. Crew or ship activities requiring extensive travel should follow the guidelines in the BSA publication *Tours and Expeditions,* No. 33737C. See "tour permit."

treasurer (crew). A Venturer elected to manage the crew's budget and the proper accounting for funds. (See Treasurer's Records in the Appendix of the *Venturing Leader Manual,* No. 34655B.)

U

ultralights. See "parachuting or hang gliding."

unauthorized activities. See "all-terrain vehicles," "boxing," "chainsaws and mechanical log-splitters," "cross-country flights," "experimental class aircraft flying," "fireworks," "flying policy," "football," "hazardous activities," "hot-air ballooning," "karate and boxing," "military policy," "motorized speed events and demolition derbies," "parachuting or hang gliding," "pilot training/rating certification in powered and nonpowered aircraft," "racing," "rodeo," "search and rescue aircraft flying," and "skin and scuba diving."

uniforms and insignia (BSA). The BSA green Venturing shirt is available for wear by Venturers and adult leaders. The green Venturing short-sleeve shirt with green shoulder loops will be worn with charcoal gray shorts or long pants as the recommended field uniform for Venturers. *Male and female Venturers should not wear the BSA tan shirt with green shoulder loops.* Existing insignia placement policies related to BSA uniforms shall apply to the green Venturing shirt. Crews choosing to wear a patch related to their specialty may do so on the right shoulder sleeve. District, division, council, and national adult leaders related to Venturing may wear the green, silver, or gold shoulder loops with the green Venturing shirt. Sea Scouts may choose to wear nautical-style uniforms using Sea Scouting insignia available from the BSA Supply Division. For further information on BSA uniforms and insignia, contact your BSA local council or refer to the *Venturer Handbook*. A uniform, if any, is the choice of the crew.

V

Venturer. A registered member of a Venturing crew.

Venturing activity interest survey. An annual survey of the career and leisure inter-

ests of high school students conducted by the local council. Survey results may be available to help crews recruit new members.

Venturing Code. As a Venturer, I believe that America's strength lies in our trust in God and in the courage, strength, and traditions of our people. I will, therefore, be faithful in my religious duties and will maintain a personal sense of honor in my own life. I will treasure my American heritage and will do all I can to preserve and enrich it. I will recognize the dignity and worth of all humanity and will use fair play and goodwill in my daily life. I will acquire the Venturing attitude that seeks truth in all things and adventure on the frontiers of our changing world.

Venturing Impact Plan. A council organizational plan to "sell" business, industry, labor, professional, church, and community groups to organize Venturing crews.

Venturing invitational events. Activities and events are hosted by some local councils for all Venturers. Venturing crews that wish to host events involving other units must have the approval of the local council. This includes events for packs, troops, teams, crews, and ships from the same council, neighboring councils, the same region, or other regions.

Guidelines: (1) The proposed unit event (pack, troop, team, crew, or ship) must contribute directly or indirectly to the strengthening of participating units' program; (2) the proposal, including a written statement of objectives of the event, must be submitted to the local council Scout executive for approval; (3) if unit(s) from councils within the same region will be involved, the Scout executive must then forward the proposal to the region for its approval; and (4) if unit(s) from other regions will be involved, the proposal must be forwarded to the appropriate division of the national office for review and approval.

Venturing leader training. Each BSA local council, through a volunteer training team, offers a variety of training opportunities to support youth and adult crew leaders.

Venturing Oath. As a Venturer, I promise to do my duty to God and help strengthen America; to help others, and to seek truth, fairness, and adventure in our world.

Venturing participation and achievement patches. Numerous patches are available from BSA local council service centers for recognizing Venturers' participation or achievement. They include Fifty-Miler Award, Historic Trails Award, Mile Swim, BSA Lifeguard, Hornaday Award, international activity patch, high-adventure emblem, Philmont Scout Ranch, religious emblem square knot, Long Cruise badge, World Crest, high-adventure bases, and Quality Unit Award.

Venturing program conference. Conducted by many councils to provide program support and training to Venturing leaders. The Advisor, associate Advisors, president, and vice presidents from each crew attend.

Y

Young American Awards. Local and national awards available to recognize young adults between the ages of 15 and 25 who have achieved excellence in the fields of art, athletics, business, community service, education, government, humanities, literature, music, religion, or science. Recipients are encouraged to be, but need not necessarily be, members of the BSA. The national Young American Awards include five unrestricted grants of $5,000. (Contact BSA local council for details.)

Youth Protection guidelines. The BSA wants to ensure that no youth becomes the victim of abuse through negligence or willful acts while participating in the Venturing program of the Boy Scouts of America. The videotape *Youth Protection Guidelines: Training for Adult Venturing Leaders,* AV-03V014, provides an overview of Youth Protection issues for adults. *Youth Protection: Personal Safety Awareness,* AV-09V027, is a presentation for any young person 14 to 20 years old.

VENTURING

SCOUTING'S NEXT STEP

BOY SCOUTS OF AMERICA